Heirloom Embroidery

JAN CONSTANTINE

Heirloom Embroidery

INSPIRED DESIGNER PROJECTS WITH BEAUTIFUL STITCHING TECHNIQUES

LARK
BOOKS

A Division of Sterling Publishing Co., Inc.
New York / London

PHOTOGRAPHY BY CAROLINE ARBER

Library of Congress Cataloging-in-Publication Data

Constantine, Jan.
 Heirloom embroidery : inspired designer projects with beautiful stitching
techniques / Jan Constantine. -- 1st ed.
    p. cm.
  Includes index.
  ISBN 978-1-60059-346-8 (HC-PLC with jkt. : alk. paper)
  1. Embroidery--Patterns. I. Title.
  TT771.C6567 2008
  746.44'041--dc22

                    2008010343

10 9 8 7 6 5 4 3 2 1

First Edition

Published by Lark Books, A Division of
Sterling Publishing Co., Inc.
387 Park Avenue South, New York, NY 10016

First published in 2008 by Jacqui Small LLP
An imprint of Aurum Press Ltd
7 Greenland Street
London NW1 0ND

Text and projects copyright © Jan Constantine 2008
Photography, illustrations, design and layout copyright © Jacqui Small 2008

Distributed in Canada by Sterling Publishing,
c/o Canadian Manda Group, 165 Dufferin Street
Toronto, Ontario, Canada M6K 3H6

If you have questions or comments about this book, please contact:
Lark Books
67 Broadway
Asheville, NC 28801
828-253-0467

Manufactured in Singapore

978-1-60059-346-8

For information about custom editions, special sales, premium and corporate
purchases, please contact Sterling Special Sales Department at 800-805-5489 or
specialsales@sterlingpub.com.

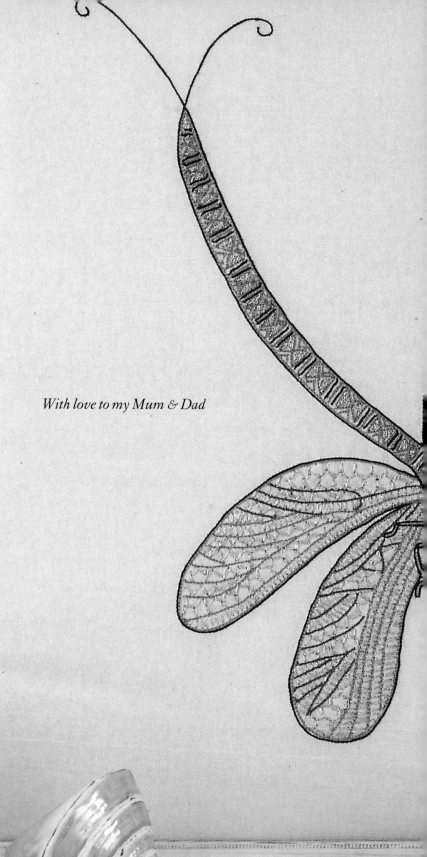

With love to my Mum & Dad

contents

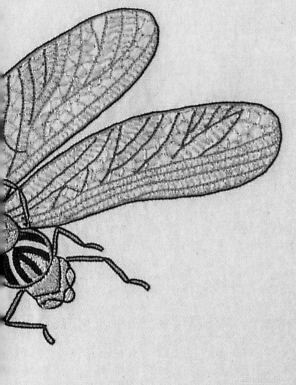

Introduction

For centuries embroidery has played a major role in our cultures and has proved to be a wonderful way to express creativity. Women used to gather together in groups to hand-work their embroidery, and while they worked, they talked and supported one another. Almost all of our grandmothers had sewing skills born out of necessity and would always have had an embroidery project on the go. They embroidered cushion covers, bed linen and table linen to be displayed as 'Sunday best' and passed on to the next generation. I hope that my book will help to inspire a passion for the art of sewing and embroidery, just as I was inspired when I was growing up.

I was born in Lancashire, the traditional home of textiles in the UK, and come from a long line of needlewomen. My grandmother was a dressmaker and milliner and my mother was a tailoress. When I was a child my parents made almost everything that I and my four siblings wore and played with. One of my first toys that had actually been bought for me was a little red sewing machine that sewed in chain stitch. I was away, in creative heaven, and I loved it, making wonderful clothes for all my dolls. My grandmother taught me to knit, crochet and embroider, and later, on my mother's sewing machine, I made every item of clothing I wore, and the highlight of my week was wearing my latest creation to the disco on Saturday night.

I went on to train in fashion and worked as designer for a large London fashion house when I qualified. I specialized in embroidered garments and had my own designer label within the company. Finding that I craved green fields, I moved to the Cheshire countryside where I established an interiors business, but I yearned to work with textiles again so began sewing lavender bags at my kitchen table with the help of friends. Since then my embroidered collections have grown and become recognized all over the world.

Heirloom Embroidery is filled with projects that I have made and loved and which others may want to make, use and hand down to future generations. The book takes you through my major collections, which have been inspired by favorite things and traditional embroidery. Starting with Hearts, this symbolic motif is intrinsic to all my work and was the starting point for my business. Its meaning is love and it is what we create when we sew a heart motif simply with blanket stitch or intricately with little loops and knots. The second chapter is Country Garden, the core of my traditional embroidery and a tribute to the last great movement in British hand-embroidery. This collection is inspired by the old surviving embroideries that were worked by my grandmother and great-aunts between the 1920s and 1950s. The third chapter, Seaside, is based on the happy times spent by the sea in the little Cornish fisherman's cottage belonging to my family. All the projects were designed and often stitched while watching the waves roll by. In the fourth chapter, Botanicals and Bugs, I explore my classical side, which adores elegance. The exquisite beauty of these designs transcends them into timeless classics, which will be appreciated for ever. Finally, Celebrations offers a variety of projects that can add the finishing touches to our festivities year after year.

Jan Constantine

Hearts

Heart Blanket and Cushions

Made from soft felted wool, this luxurious blanket and matching cushions feature a striking appliqué heart design. This is a fairly quick project to make – for novices as well as experienced embroiderers – as blanket stitch is one of the easiest stitches to master, while the felted wool doesn't fray, so the edges can be left raw.

Blanket

Materials and equipment

- 1¾ yds (160cm) of red wool felt (minimum 52 in/130cm wide) for the blanket
- 15¾ in (40cm) of cream wool felt for the contrasting appliqué hearts
- Bonding web
- Heart design templates for the central and four corner hearts (see page 13)
- Sharp, hard pencil
- Embroidery kit and stranded cotton embroidery thread (dyefast) in both the main (red) and contrasting (cream) colors
- Sewing machine, thread and sewing kit
- Ironing cloth

Stitches

Blanket stitch appliqué and blanket stitch edging (see page 12).

Preparation and cutting out

Prepare the fabric by pressing (see tips on page 126). Referring to the notes on page 127, cut the blanket to size. This blanket is 1¾ yds (160cm) long and has been cut out from the whole width of the fabric (52 in/130cm), with the selvedges trimmed off.

Using a photocopier, enlarge the heart pattern on page 13 so that it measures 13⅞ in (35cm) in width. This template is for the large heart in the center of the blanket. Make a template for the four corner hearts, using the pattern at full size, as shown.

Appliqué embroidery

Trace one large heart and four small hearts onto a sheet of bonding web using a sharp pencil. Following the manufacturer's instructions, iron the bonding web onto the wrong side of the contrasting cream wool fabric (see picture 1).

Cut out the heart shapes neatly on the inside of the line and peel off the bonding web backing (see picture 2).

Place the large heart shape in the center of the blanket, right side up. Then pin a small heart in each of the four corners, with the points of the hearts to the corners and 3¼ in (8cm) in. Pin in place and iron to fuse the fabrics together, using a cloth to protect the wool and prevent the hot iron from making it shiny (see picture 3).

Using six strands of red thread (or the same color as your blanket), work blanket stitch round the outline of the large central appliquéd heart and the four corner hearts (see picture 4). Stitch neatly and evenly and size the stitches according to the size of the heart, using larger stitches and wider spacing for the larger heart and smaller stitches closer together for the smaller hearts.

Making up the blanket

Tack and then machine stitch a neat ½-in (1cm) hem all round the blanket. Sew another parallel line of machine stitching on the very edge of the blanket.

Embroider the edges with blanket stitch using cream thread (or the same color as your appliquéd heart shapes), following the inner machine-stitched line and spacing the stitches ½ in (1cm) apart (see picture 5).

Finishing

Press lightly with a damp cloth.

Blanket stitch appliqué

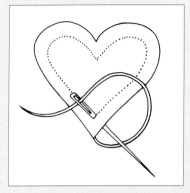 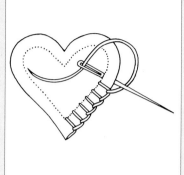

With the heart shape securely in place, mark an inner stitch guideline with tailor's chalk and work from left to right. Bring the needle to the front of the main fabric, just below the lower point of the heart. Put the needle into the heart on the upper marked line, one space to the right and straight out again, just below the front edge, over the top of the working thread. Continue as required, spacing the stitches evenly along the row so that they are symmetrical on both sides of the heart.

Blanket stitch edging

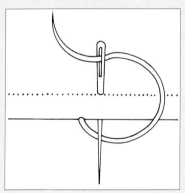 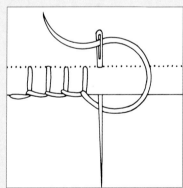

Mark a stitch guideline parallel to the edge. Working from left to right, bring the needle out to the front of the fabric very close to the edge. Put the needle in on the upper line, one space to the right, and bring it through to the front again over the top of the working thread. Continue as required, spacing the stitches evenly along the row. To finish, secure the thread by making a tiny stitch on the edge.

heart blanket template

LARGE CENTRAL HEART
Enlarge the template to 13⅞ in (35cm) width.
Cut 1 in cream wool felt and position in the center
of the blanket.

SMALL CORNER HEARTS
Use at full size, as shown.
Cut 4 in cream wool felt and position in each
corner of the blanket with the point 3¼ in (8cm)
from the corner.

HEART BLANKET
Position the hearts as in the diagram below.
Final blanket size 63 x 52 in (160 x 130cm).

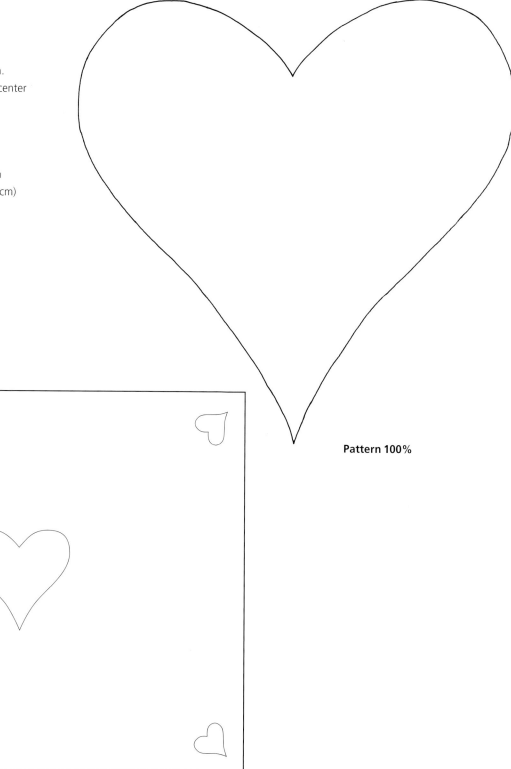

Pattern 100%

Cushion

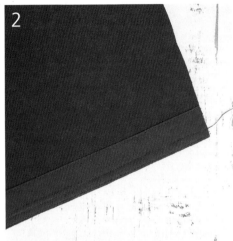

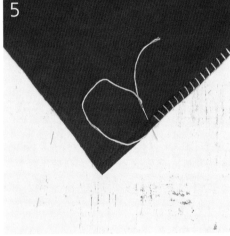

Materials and equipment

- ⅝ yd (50cm) of red wool felt (minimum 52 in/130cm wide) for the cushion
- 15 x 15 in (30 x 30cm) of cream wool felt for the contrasting appliqué hearts
- Two 1⅝ x 17¾ in (4 x 45cm) pieces of cotton for the back opening facings
- 11⅞ x 11⅞ in (30 x 30cm) of bonding web
- 3⅞ in (10cm) of iron-on interfacing
- Two buttons, ⅞ in (2cm) diameter
- Heart design template (see page 15)
- Cushion pattern (see pages 32–3)
- Sharp, hard pencil
- 15 x 15 in (38 x 38cm) feather-filled cushion inner
- Embroidery kit and stranded cotton embroidery thread (dyefast) in both the main (red) and contrasting (cream) colors
- Sewing machine, thread and sewing kit
- Ironing cloth

Stitches

Blanket stitch appliqué and blanket stitch edging (see page 12), plus buttonhole stitch for the buttonholes (see page 123) or use the sewing machine.

Preparation and cutting out

Prepare the wool felt fabric by pressing, see tips on page 126.

Using a photocopier, enlarge the heart pattern opposite so that it measures 6¾ in (17cm) in width. This template is for the large heart on the front of the cushion. Make a template for the small heart for the back of the cushion, using the pattern at full size, as shown. Enlarge the cushion pattern to full size, shown on pages 32–3 at 50 percent.

Referring to the notes on cutting out on page 127, cut out one cushion front and two cushion backs in wool felt. Cut out two back facings in cotton and two in iron-on interfacing.

Appliqué embroidery

Following the instructions for the Heart Blanket (see pages 11–12), trace one large heart and one small heart onto bonding web using a sharp pencil. Iron the bonding web onto the wrong side of the contrasting cream wool felt and carefully cut out the heart shapes.

Peel off the bonding web backing and pin the large heart onto the center of the cushion front piece, right side up, and the small one onto the center of the top cushion back piece, with the point 1½ in (4cm) from the edge. Using an ironing cloth, iron to fuse the heart shapes to the cushion pieces.

Using six strands of red thread (or the color of the cushion), outline the large appliquéd heart and then the small heart with blanket stitch, working neat, even stitches and sizing them according to the size of the heart motif – use larger stitches and wider spacing for the larger heart and much smaller ones for the small heart.

Making up the cushion

Press iron-on interfacing to the wrong side of the cotton back facing. Turn the outer edge under by ½ in (5mm) and press the hem in place (see picture 1).

With right sides together, pin, tack and machine stitch the facing to one of the wool felt cushion back pieces, sewing a ½-in (1cm) seam along the edge. Press the seam open, then fold back onto the wrong side of the cushion and press. Pin, tack and machine a line of stitching 1⅜ in (3.5cm) from the edge to hold the facing in place. Machine two parallel lines of stitching, one on the edge and the other ½ in (1cm) away from the edge (see picture 2).

Repeat this process for the other cushion back piece and facing.

Mark two buttonhole positions on the wrong side of the upper cushion back piece, ⅞ in (2cm) above the edge and 3⅞ in (10cm) apart. Work two 1-in (2.5cm) buttonholes by machine or by hand.

Work blanket stitch along the edge of the opening with cream thread (or the color of the contrasting hearts), following the inner machine-stitched line and spacing the stitches ½ in (1cm) apart.

Lay the upper back piece over the top edge of the lower back piece, matching up the balance points at the sides. Sew two buttons onto the lower cushion back at the marked points, corresponding with the buttonholes on the upper piece (see picture 3).

Do up the buttons and tack both sides of the back piece to secure.

With wrong sides together, pin the front and back of the cushion together, then tack and machine stitch ½-in (1cm) seams round all four edges. Machine a parallel stitch line along the outer edge (see picture 4).

Finally, use six strands of cream thread (or the color of the contrasting hearts) to edge the cushion with blanket stitch. Work neat stitches using the inner stitch line as a guide and spacing them ½ in (1cm) apart (see picture 5).

Finishing

Lightly press the finished cushion cover with a slightly damp cloth between the fabric and the iron to prevent it from becoming shiny.

heart cushion template

LARGE FRONT HEART
Enlarge the template to 6¾ in (17cm) width. Cut 1 in cream wool felt and position in the center of the front piece of the cushion.

SMALL BACK HEART
Use at full size, as shown. Cut 1 in cream wool felt and position in the center of the top back piece , with the point 1⅝ in (4cm) from the edge.

Pattern 100%

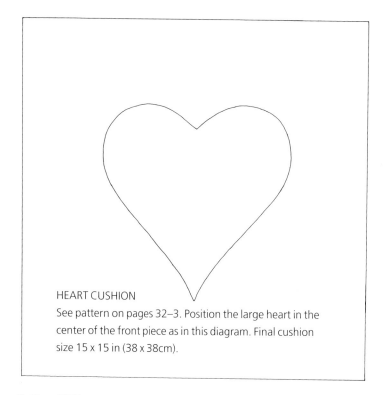

HEART CUSHION
See pattern on pages 32–3. Position the large heart in the center of the front piece as in this diagram. Final cushion size 15 x 15 in (38 x 38cm).

Pattern 25%

Heart Laundry Bag

This useful and attractive laundry bag, decorated with three appliquéd hearts, is a very simple and satisfying project to stitch. The bag can be hung up in the bedroom or bathroom, and could easily be made in a smaller size and used as a shoebag.

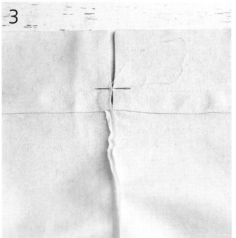

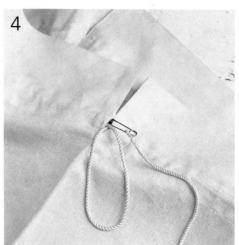

Materials and equipment

- ⅞ yd (80cm) of white or cream linen or linen/cotton mix (minimum 47 in/120cm wide)
- Red wool, cotton or linen (dyefast) for the appliqué hearts
- Bonding web
- Two 1½-yd (140cm) lengths of white cord for the drawstring, ⅛ in (3mm) wide
- Heart design template (see page 18)
- Laundry bag pattern (see page 19)
- Sharp, hard pencil
- Masking tape
- Embroidery kit and stranded cotton embroidery thread (dyefast) in cream
- Sewing machine, thread and sewing kit
- Safety pin to thread cord through the casing

Stitches

Blanket stitch appliqué (see page 18).

Preparation and cutting out

Prepare the wool felt fabric for embroidery (see tips on page 126).

Make a template of the heart pattern, shown at full size on page 18. Using a photocopier, enlarge the laundry bag pattern to full size, shown on page 19 at 25 percent. Referring to the notes on page 127, cut out two pieces in linen for the bag.

Appliqué embroidery

Following the instructions for the Heart Blanket (see pages 11–12), trace three heart shapes onto

bonding web using a sharp pencil. Iron the bonding web onto the wrong side of the felt and cut out the hearts. Peel off the backing and pin the hearts onto the right side of the front piece of the bag, 2¼ in (5.5cm) apart and with the points 3⅜ in (8.5cm) from the bottom edge. Iron the back to fuse the fabrics.

Use six strands of cream thread to outline the appliquéd hearts with blanket stitch. Stitch neatly with ¼-in-long (6mm) stitches every ¼ in (6mm).

Making up

Place the front and back pieces of the bag with right sides together. Pin, tack and machine stitch a ½-in (1cm) seam along the bottom and sides, starting and finishing at the first set of balance points. Neaten the raw edges of the seam with zigzag stitch. Turn the bag right side out and press. Turn the top edge in by ¼ in (5mm) and press.

To prepare the channel for the drawstrings, work on the front and back sections separately. Fold the flap at the fold line marked on the pattern, so the fabric is right side to right side, and pin at the side seams. Tack, then machine-stitch a ½-in (1cm) seam from the second balance point upwards to form the 2¾-in (7cm) frill (see picture 1).

Turn this section right side out. Then, making sure the ¼-in (5mm) pressed hem is turned under, pin, tack and machine stitch along the edge (see picture 2). Then machine another parallel line 1 in (2.5cm) above this to form the drawstring channel.

Repeat this on the other side of the bag opening. Then, working on the inside of the bag, join the front and back together at the top of the drawstring gap by firmly overstitching by hand (see picture 3).

Finishing
Press the bag lightly (see notes on page 128).

Thread one piece of cord through the channel with a safety pin and stitch the ends together. Pull the cord round to hide the join inside the casing. Repeat with the other piece of cord, threading it through from the other side (see picture 4). Pull both cords at opposite sides of the casing, closing the bag and forming handles.

laundry bag heart template

Pattern 100%

Blanket stitch appliqué

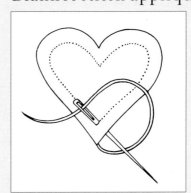 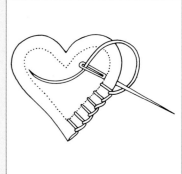

With the heart shape securely in place, mark an inner stitch guideline and work from left to right. Bring the needle to the front of the main fabric, just below the lower point of the heart. Put the needle into the heart on the upper marked line, one space to the right and straight out again, just below the front edge, over the top of the working thread. Continue as required, spacing the stitches evenly along the row so that they are symmetrical on both sides of the heart.

laundry bag template

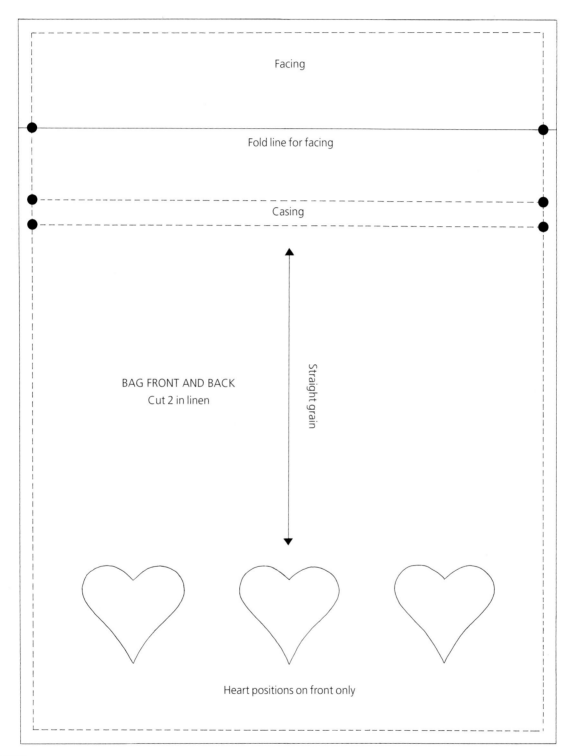

Facing

Fold line for facing

Casing

BAG FRONT AND BACK
Cut 2 in linen

Straight grain

Heart positions on front only

Pattern 25%

Heart Table Runner and Napkins

These deep-red hearts embroidered onto crisp, white linen were inspired by a delicate Swedish wreath made from filigree silver wire. The stitches are relatively simple, but they need an experienced embroiderer as they are so fine and dainty.

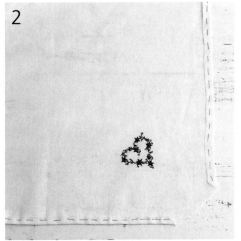

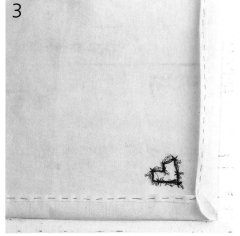

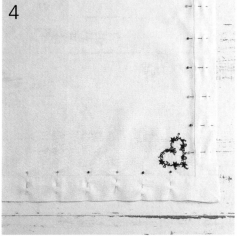

Materials and equipment

- Approximately 67 x 23⅝ in (170 x 60cm) of white linen for the table runner
- Approximately 23⅝ x 23⅝ in (60 x 60cm) of white linen for each napkin
  (Extra fabric allowance has been made for the embroidery to be worked and once completed the fabric will be cut to the size of the pattern)
- Heart design templates (see page 23)
- Napkin and table runner patterns (see page 23)
- Dressmaker's carbon paper
- Sharp, hard pencil
- Masking tape
- 6-in (15cm) and 10-in (25cm) embroidery rings
- Embroidery kit and stranded cotton embroidery thread (dyefast) in deep red
- Sewing machine, thread and sewing kit

Stitches

Chain stitch, French knot and loop stitch (page 22).

Preparation and cutting out

Wash the linen and iron while still damp to reduce shrinkage (see tips on page 126).

Using a photocopier, enlarge the central heart design for the table runner and the corner pattern for the napkin and runner to full size, both shown on page 23 at 50 percent.

Using these patterns and referring to the notes on page 127, cut out the table runner and your chosen number of napkins. The table runner should measure 62½ x 19 in (158 x 48cm) (finished size 59 x 15½ in/150 x 40cm) and each napkin should measure 23 x 23 in (58 x 58cm) (finished size 19½ x 19½ in/50 x 50cm).

Tracing the design

Trace the designs onto the linen fabric as follows. Working on a smooth, clean surface, place the dressmaker's carbon paper face down on the linen. Position the heart design template on top and hold it in place with masking tape. Using a sharp pencil, carefully trace over the design, checking to make sure that it is transferring clearly (see picture 1).

For each napkin, position the small heart template in one corner of the cut square, 3⅝ in (9cm) from each edge, with the point of the heart towards the corner.

For the table runner, use the same small heart template in all four corners and position the large design in the center of the runner, straight on the grain of the fabric, as on the diagram on page 23.

Loop stitch

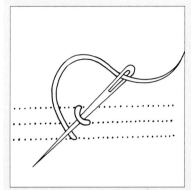 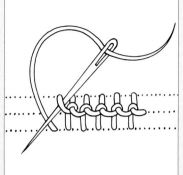

This is used as a straight line to emphasize the wide hem of the napkins and the runner. Mark two parallel lines above and below the hem. Working from right to left, bring the needle up in the center,

put the needle in on the top line and out on the lower line, slightly to the left. Take the needle under the previous stitch from right to left and then over the top of the thread to form the loop. Repeat as required.

French knot

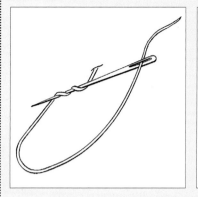 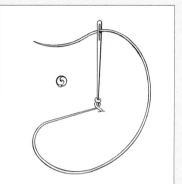

Bring the thread up through the fabric, hold it with the thumb and first finger of the left hand and turn the needle round it once or twice, or as necessary.

Still holding the thread firmly with the left hand, turn the needle and insert it close to the point at which it

emerged (not exactly the same place or it will just pull back through). Pull the thread taut so that the knot slides down the needle to touch the fabric. Release the thread as the needle goes through the fabric with the knot remaining on the surface.

Chain stitch

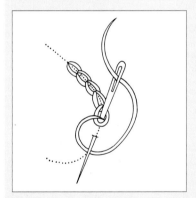

One of the oldest and most widely used stitches, chain stitch is used as an outline or a filling stitch by working multiple rows.

Work the chain downwards making a series of loops the same size and not too tight or they will lose their shape. Bring the needle out to the front of the fabric and return it through the same point, bringing it out again to cover the working thread with the needle, forming a loop. Repeat as required and finish the last loop with a tiny straight stitch.

Embroidery

Work the embroidery for the corner hearts using a 6-in (15cm) embroidery ring, stretching the fabric well and securing the ring firmly to keep it taut. Then work the larger heart design on the table runner using a 10-in (25cm) embroidery ring.

Both the table runner and napkins are embroidered in deep red thread, as follows:

• Stitch the outline of the hearts in chain stitch using three strands.

• Work the outlines of the flowers and leaves in chain stitch using one strand.

• Fill in the larger flowers with chain stitch, following the outline and working towards the middle of each petal, using one strand.

• Work the outlines of the vines and tendrils with one row of fine chain stitch using one strand.

• Finish with clusters of three or four French knots inside the larger flowers and individual French knots spaced randomly round the outlines using six strands.

• For the smaller French knots on the smaller heart on the napkin, use four strands.

Making up

For the edges of the runner and napkins, turn a ½-in (1cm) hem towards the right side, tack and press (see picture 2).

To form the miter on each corner, with wrong sides together, fold in the edges by 1¼ in (3cm) and bring the two corners together, matching the two points, to form a right angle. Pin, tack and machine stitch the corners together (see picture 3).

Press the corner seam open and turn the mitered corner through. Then pin, tack and machine stitch all round the edges to form the 1¼ in- (3cm)-wide hem (see picture 4).

Finishing

Following the stitch line on the hem, embroider loop stitch in deep red to finish.

Press the table runner and napkins on the reverse side, making sure that the French knots are not flattened by the pressure of the iron (see notes on pressing and finishing on page 128).

heart table runner and napkins template

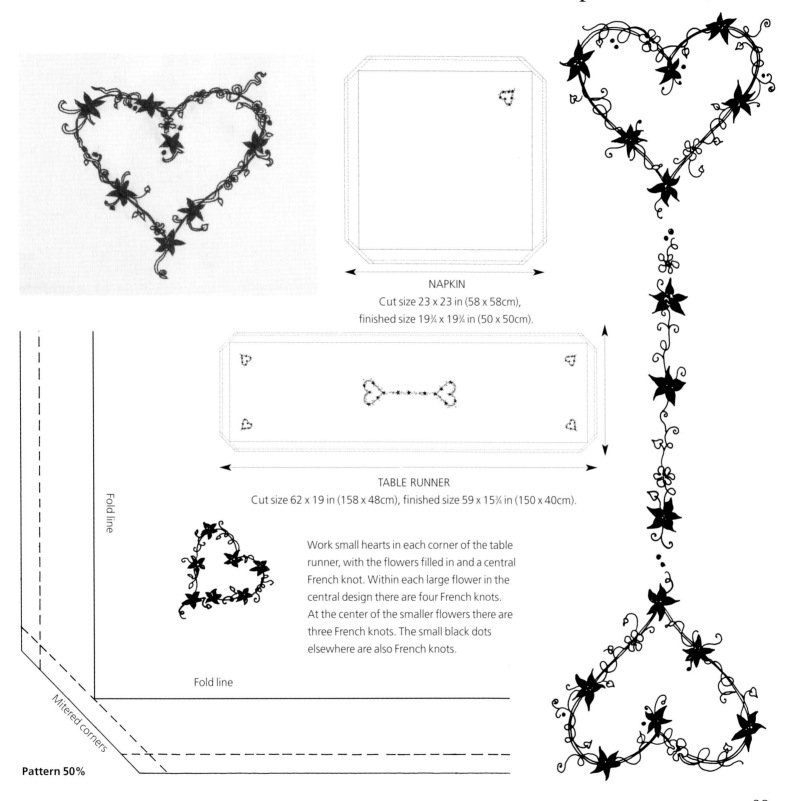

NAPKIN
Cut size 23 x 23 in (58 x 58cm),
finished size 19¾ x 19¾ in (50 x 50cm).

TABLE RUNNER
Cut size 62 x 19 in (158 x 48cm), finished size 59 x 15¾ in (150 x 40cm).

Fold line

Fold line

Mitered corners

Work small hearts in each corner of the table runner, with the flowers filled in and a central French knot. Within each large flower in the central design there are four French knots. At the center of the smaller flowers there are three French knots. The small black dots elsewhere are also French knots.

Pattern 50%

Heart Apron

This pretty heart apron is very feminine, with a flattering sweetheart neckline and the striking embroidery on the bodice. It's the perfect apron for looking good in the kitchen.

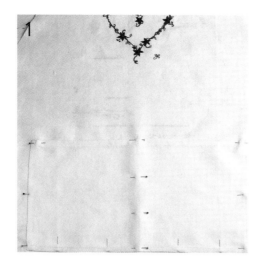

Stitches

Chain stitch and French knot, as on the Heart Table Runner and Napkins (see page 22).

Preparation and cutting out

Wash the linen fabric and iron while still damp to reduce shrinkage (see tips on page 126).

Using a photocopier, enlarge the heart design template to full size, shown on page 27 at 50 percent. Enlarge the apron and neck facing patterns to full size, shown on page 27 at 25 percent. Referring to the notes on page 127, pin the neck facing and apron pattern onto the linen and draw round it with tailor's chalk, adding 2 in (5cm) round the bodice to secure the embroidery ring (you will cut out the bodice when the embroidery is complete). Cut out the shapes. Cut out two waist ties, 43 x 2⅞ in (110 x 7.5cm), one neck band, 52 x 7.5 in (52 x 7.5cm), and one pocket, 16½ x 9 in (42 x 23cm).

Tracing the design

Working on a smooth, clean surface, place the dressmaker's carbon paper face down on the apron bodice and position the heart design template centrally on top, 2 in (5cm) down from the top edge of the apron. Make sure it is straight on the grain of the fabric and attach it with masking tape. Using a sharp pencil, carefully trace round the design, checking to make sure that it is transferring clearly (see picture 1 on page 20).

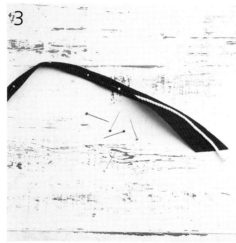

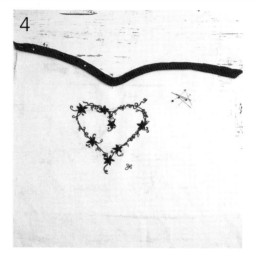

Embroidery

Work the embroidery for the heart using a 10-in (25cm) embroidery ring, stretching the fabric well and securing it firmly. The heart is embroidered throughout in deep red thread, as follows:

• Stitch the outline of the heart in chain stitch using three strands.

• Work the outlines of the flowers and leaves in chain stitch using one strand.

• Fill in the larger flowers with chain stitch, following the outline and working towards the middle of each petal, using one strand.

• Work the outlines of the vines and tendrils with two rows of fine chain stitch using one strand.

• Finish with clusters of three or four French knots

Materials and equipment

• 1⅛-yd (100cm) length of white linen or linen/cotton mix
• Heart design template (see page 27)
• Apron pattern (see page 27)
• 15¾ in (40cm) of cotton piping cord, ⅛ in (3mm) wide
• 11¼ x 11¼ in (30 x 30cm) of red cotton (dyefast) for the contrasting piping
• Tailor's chalk
• Metal ruler
• Dressmaker's carbon paper
• Masking tape
• Sharp, hard pencil
• 10-in (25cm) embroidery ring
• Embroidery kit and stranded cotton embroidery thread (dyefast) in deep red
• Sewing machine, thread and sewing kit

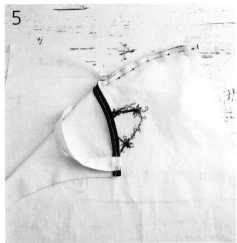

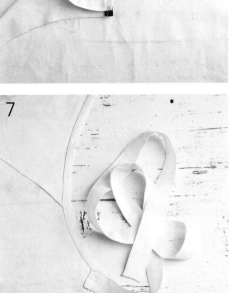

inside the larger flowers and individual French knots spaced quite randomly round the outline. This produces a lovely texture.

Making up

Cut the apron bodice to size, using the pattern.

To hem the top edge of the pocket, turn over ¼ in (5mm), pin and press. Turn over another ½ in (1cm) and pin, tack and machine stitch two rows of stitching, one on the edge and one ⅜ in (8mm) in from the edge. Fold in ½ in (1cm) along the other three edges of the pocket and pin, tack and press.

Position the pocket on the front of the apron, following the pattern, and pin, tack and machine stitch it in place along the sides and bottom.

Stitch a vertical line through the center of the pocket from the top to the bottom edge to divide it in half. Remove all the tacking thread once the machine stitching is complete (see picture 1).

Make up the neck band by folding the strip of fabric in half lengthways, and then pin, tack and machine stitch a ½-in (1cm) seam down the long edge, leaving both ends open. Turn through to the right side and press flat.

Repeat to make the two waist ties, closing them at both ends and pressing as before.

For the piped insertion edging on the neckline, cut out a bias strip in contrasting red dyefast cotton. To do this, fold the 11¼ in (30cm) square of fabric diagonally so that one corner meets the other to form a triangle. Cut along the fold line. Using tailor's chalk, mark a parallel line 1¼ in (3cm) from the cut edge and cut along this line to create a 1¼ in- (3cm)-wide strip of fabric (see picture 2).

To make the piping cord, fold the bias strip in half over the piping cord and pin, tack and machine stitch close to the piping (see picture 3).

Pin the piping along the seam line to the front of the apron neckline (see picture 4). When stitching round the V shape, lift the presser foot slightly with the needle through the fabric and swivel the fabric to change direction, then lower the presser foot and continue stitching.

Hem the bottom of the facing in the same way as the top edge of the pocket, first turning over ¼ in (5mm) and pinning and pressing, then turning over another ½ in (1cm) and pinning, tacking and machine stitching two rows of stitching, one on the edge and one ⅜ in (8mm) in from the edge.

Before attaching the facing, pin and tack the ends of the neck band onto each edge of the neckline with right sides together, and stitch in place. With right sides together, pin, tack and machine stitch the facing to the neckline of the apron (see picture 5).

Turn through to the right side of the apron and machine stitch the edge of the neckline to give a crisp finish (see picture 6).

Hem all round the apron, first folding in ¼ in (5mm) then folding in another ½ in (1cm), as described for the top edge of the pocket.

Attach the waist ties to the wrong side of the apron, as marked on the pattern, overlapping the ends by 1 in (2.5cm) and pinning then tacking them in place. Sew a square on the machine and then sew from corner to corner to form a cross and keep the ties secure (see picture 7).

Finishing

Press the apron on the reverse side, making sure that the French knots are not flattened by the pressure of the iron (see notes on pressing and finishing on page 128).

heart apron template

Piped neckline

Neck band

Hems: ¼ in (5mm) and
½ in (1cm) turn-ins

Waist ties

Pocket position

Center front fold line

APRON FRONT – Place on fold and cut 1 in linen

Straight grain

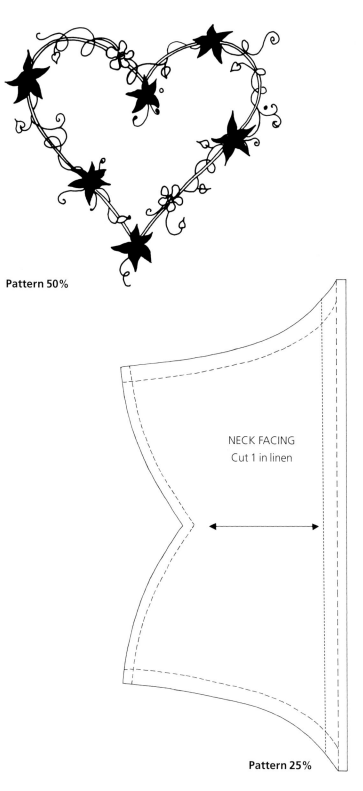

Pattern 50%

NECK FACING
Cut 1 in linen

Pattern 25%

Country Garden

Daisy Bag

Always fresh and modern, the daisy has been a favorite motif for centuries in many cultures. This useful bag is very satisfying to stitch and looks super-stylish.

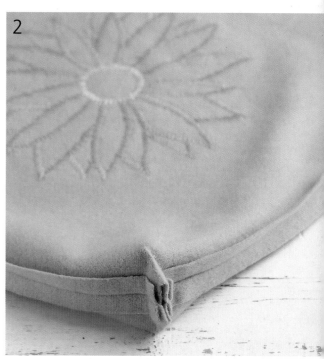

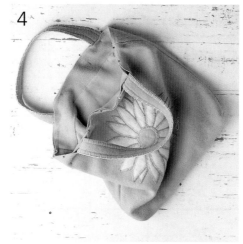

Materials and equipment

- 15¾ in (40cm) of green wool felt for the bag
- 9⅞ x 9⅞ in (25 x 25cm) of cream wool felt for the daisy
- 2 x 2 in (5 x 5cm) of yellow wool felt for the center
- 11¾ in (30cm) of green cotton for the lining
- Bonding web
- Daisy design template (see page 36)
- Bag and lining patterns (see pages 36–7)
- Dressmaker's carbon paper
- Sharp, hard pencil
- Embroidery kit and stranded cotton embroidery thread (dyefast) in green, yellow and cream
- Sewing machine, thread and sewing kit
- Ironing cloth

Stitches
Blanket stitch appliqué and blanket stitch edging (see page 122).

Preparation and cutting out
Prepare the wool fabric by pressing (see page 126).

Using a photocopier, enlarge the daisy design template and the bag and lining patterns to full size, shown on pages 36–7 at 40 percent.

Referring to the notes on cutting out on page 127, cut out one front bag piece, one back piece, two facings and four handles in green wool felt.

Then cut out one front and one back lining in green cotton.

Appliqué embroidery
Following the instructions for the heart blanket (see pages 11–12), trace the outline of the daisy petals onto a piece of bonding web using a sharp pencil. Iron the bonding web onto the wrong side of the cream wool felt. Trace the daisy center onto another piece of bonding web and iron the bonding web to the wrong side of the yellow wool felt. Cut out the daisy petals and center.

Peel the bonding web backing off the petals and daisy center and pin them, right sides up, onto the center of the front piece of the bag, positioning the petals 2⅜ in (6cm) down from top of the bag. Iron to fuse the fabrics together using an ironing cloth to protect the wool felt from the hot iron.

Using dressmaker's carbon paper and a sharp pencil, trace the stitch guidelines for the petals onto the front of the daisy.

The daisy motif is embroidered in blanket stitch, using six strands of thread, as follows:

• Outline the appliquéd daisy petals with blanket stitch in bright green (or the color of the bag), following the traced lines and spacing the stitches approximately ⅛ in (3mm) apart.

• Blanket stitch round the daisy center in yellow.

Making up

Place the front and back pieces of the bag with right sides together and pin, tack and machine stitch a ½-in (1cm) seam along both sides and along the bottom (see picture 1). Press the seams open.

To form the gusset, with right sides together, arrange the bottom corners of the bag so that the seams at point A and B match and the edges are level. Tack and machine stitch ½ in (1cm) across the corners of the bag base (see picture 2). Turn the bag right side out.

With right sides together, pin, tack and machine stitch a ½-in (1cm) seam to join the two bag facings to the top edges of the front and back pieces of the lining. Press the seams open and make up the lining in the same way as the bag (see picture 3).

To make the bag handles, place two strips with wrong sides together and pin, tack and machine stitch a ½-in (1cm) seam along both long edges. Then sew a parallel line of stitching close to the

daisy bag template

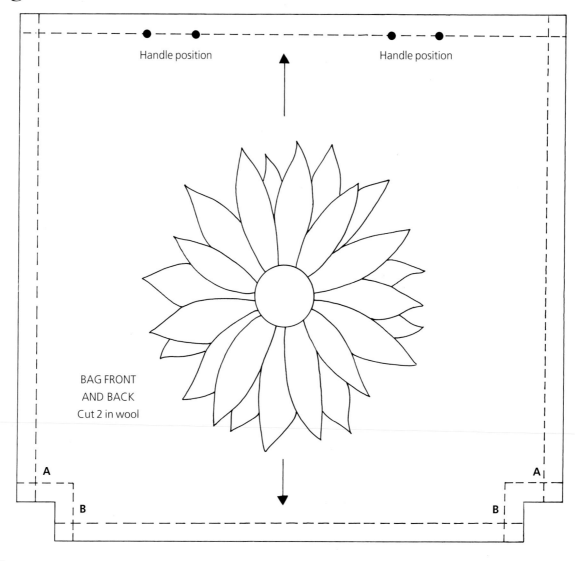

Handle position   Handle position

BAG FRONT
AND BACK
Cut 2 in wool

A

B

A

B

Pattern 40%

edges. Repeat for the second handle.

Work blanket stitch in cream thread (or the color of the contrasting daisy) along both sides of each handle. Use the inner machine-stitched line as a guide and space the stitches ½ in (1cm) apart.

Insert the lining into the bag with wrong sides facing each other. Pin the top edges together, inserting the bag handles between the two layers of fabric at the marked balance points. Pin, tack and machine stitch a ½-in (1cm) seam along the top edge, then sew a parallel line of stitching close to the edge (see picture 4).

Finally, work blanket stitch round the top edge of the bag using six strands of cream thread (or the color of the contrasting daisy). Use the machine-stitched lines to guide you and space the stitches ½ in (1cm) apart (see picture 5).

Finishing

Lightly press the finished bag (see notes on pressing and finishing on page 128).

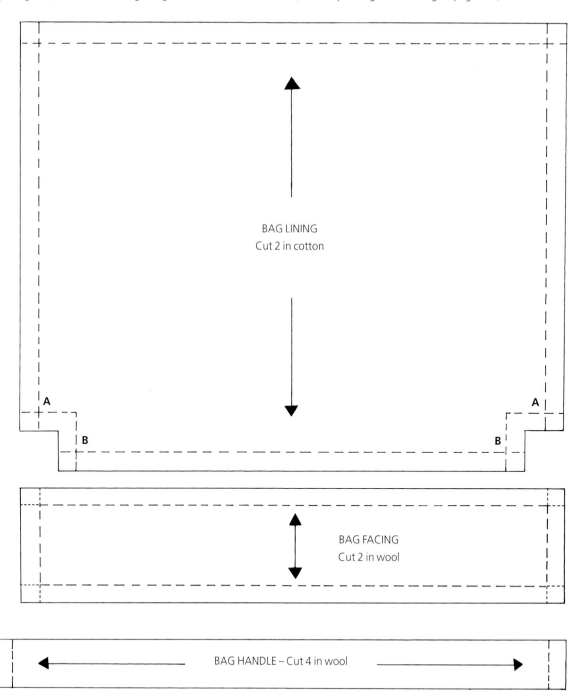

Pattern 40%

BAG LINING
Cut 2 in cotton

A   A
B   B

BAG FACING
Cut 2 in wool

BAG HANDLE – Cut 4 in wool

Pattern 40%

Strawberry Tablecloth and Napkins

Stitch these luscious strawberries onto a linen tablecloth and napkins to capture the essence of midsummer. The dainty and intricate stitches are topped with tactile French knots, which are irresistible to the touch.

Stitches

Stem stitch, chain stitch, straight stitch, satin stitch and French knot (see page 40).

Preparation

Wash and iron the linen tablecloth and napkins to reduce shrinkage (see tips on page 126).

Using a photocopier, enlarge the strawberry design templates to full size, shown on page 41 at 50 percent.

Tracing the design

Working on a smooth, clean surface, place the dressmaker's carbon paper face down on the fabric and place the template on top. Make sure it is straight on the grain of the fabric and attach it with masking tape. Using a sharp pencil, carefully trace round the design, checking to make sure that it is transferring clearly (see picture 1 of the Heart Table Runner and Napkins on page 20).

The tablecloth has the large strawberry tendril design positioned 5⅞ in (15cm) from each corner and the four small individual strawberries positioned 6¾ in (17cm) from the center of the tablecloth, facing in random directions.

The napkins each have a small single strawberry design positioned 2¾ in (7cm) from one corner.

Embroidery

Using a 10-in (25cm) embroidery ring for the tablecloth and a 6-in (15cm) ring for the napkins, stretching the fabric well and securing the rings firmly, work the embroidery as follows:

• Work the outline of the stems and tendrils in chain stitch using one strand of dark green.
• Fill in the stems and tendrils with stem stitch using three strands of bright green.
• Outline all the leaves in chain stitch using two strands of dark green.
• For the large leaf inner detail, use two strands of dark green to work the main veins in chain stitch. For the other leaf veins, work straight stitch in dark green, olive green and bright green alternately.
• Work the highlights on the large leaves in chain stitch with two strands of bright green, following the outline on the right-hand side of each leaf.
• Infill the strawberry leaves with satin stitch, using two strands of olive green for the tips of the leaves and bright green for the rest.
• Stitch the outline of the strawberry with chain stitch using two strands of dark red.
• Stitch the inner strawberry with chain stitch, using two strands to work up and down in red and randomly add a few areas of deep pink.
• Finish off the strawberry with French knots using eight strands of yellow.

Finishing

Press the tablecloth and napkins on the reverse side (see notes on pressing and finishing on page 128).

Materials and equipment

• One ready-made white linen tablecloth, approximately 39⅜ x 39⅜ in (100 x 100cm) (to make your own, follow the instructions for the Heart Table Runner and Napkins on page 20, adjusting the size of the runner accordingly)
• Six ready-made white linen napkins, approximately 19½ x 19½ in (50 x 50cm)
• Strawberry design templates (see page 41)
• Dressmaker's carbon paper
• Sharp, hard pencil
• Masking tape
• 6-in (15cm) and 10-in (25cm) embroidery rings
• Embroidery kit and stranded cotton embroidery thread (dyefast) in dark green, bright green and olive green, dark red, deep pink and yellow

Chain stitch

One of the oldest and most widely used stitches, chain stitch is used as an outline or a filling stitch by working multiple rows.

Work the chain downwards making a series of loops the same size and not too tight or they will lose their shape. Bring the needle out to the front of the fabric and return it through the same point, bringing it out again to cover the working thread with the needle, forming a loop. Repeat as required and finish the last loop with a tiny straight stitch.

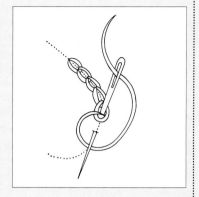

Stem stitch

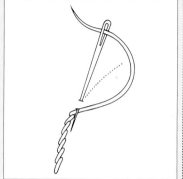

Working from left to right, bring the needle out to the front of the fabric and, slanting a little, put the needle in to the right and bring it back out halfway along the working stitch. Continue as required.

Straight stitch

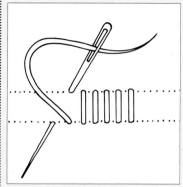

Used for short straight lines, work regularly, as shown, or randomly.

Bring the needle to the front of the fabric and put it back in directly above. Repeat and work consistently, with the needle always going in at the top and back out at the bottom.

Satin stitch

Satin stitch creates a smooth filling for small areas such as flowers and leaves.

The tension must be kept even and the stitches quite short to keep them neat.

Work straight stitches next to each other, taking the needle through as shown and repeating consistently for a smooth and even finish, with no background fabric visible.

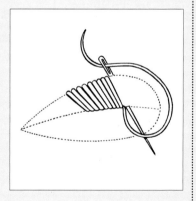

French knot

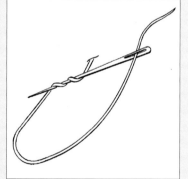

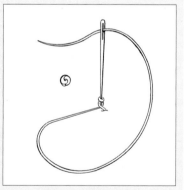

Bring the thread up through the fabric, hold it with the thumb and first finger of the left hand and turn the needle round it once or twice, or as necessary.

Still holding the thread firmly with the left hand, turn the needle and insert it close to the point at which

it emerged (not exactly the same place or it will just pull back through). Pull the thread taut so that the knot slides down the needle to touch the fabric. Release the thread as the needle goes through the fabric with the knot remaining on the surface.

strawberry tablecloth and napkins template

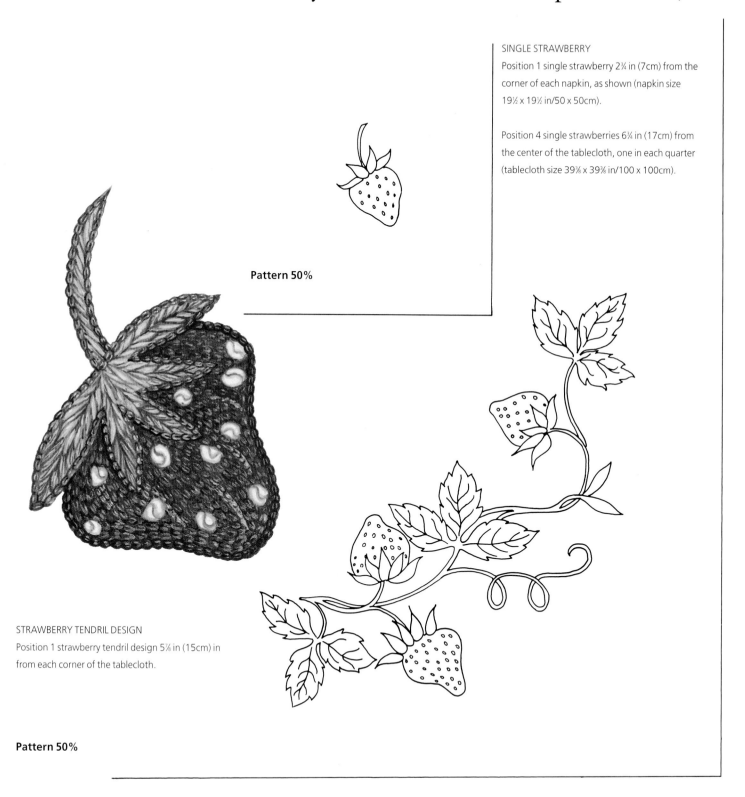

SINGLE STRAWBERRY
Position 1 single strawberry 2¾ in (7cm) from the corner of each napkin, as shown (napkin size 19½ x 19½ in/50 x 50cm).

Position 4 single strawberries 6¾ in (17cm) from the center of the tablecloth, one in each quarter (tablecloth size 39⅜ x 39⅜ in/100 x 100cm).

Pattern 50%

STRAWBERRY TENDRIL DESIGN
Position 1 strawberry tendril design 5⅞ in (15cm) in from each corner of the tablecloth.

Pattern 50%

Strawberry Lavender Sachet

A single strawberry, my favorite fruit, adorns this lavender sachet with its smart red scalloped edges. The inner sachet can be refilled, as required, to keep the fragrance fresh.

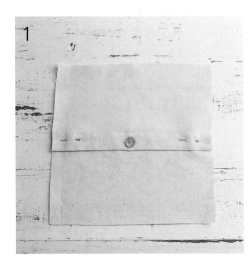

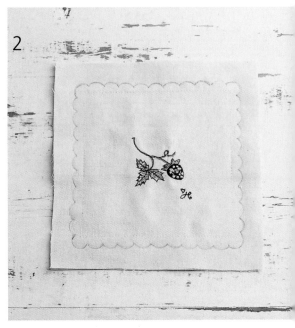

Materials and equipment
- 7⅞ in (20cm) of cream linen
- 5⅞ in (15cm) of white or cream muslin
- 13⅞ in (35cm) of cream or red satin ribbon, ⅛ in (3mm) wide
- 1 button, ⅝ in (1.5cm) diameter
- 2.5 oz (70g) of fragrant loose lavender
- Strawberry design template (see page 45)
- Sachet pattern (see page 45)
- Dressmaker's carbon paper
- Sharp, hard pencil
- Masking tape
- Embroidery kit and stranded cotton embroidery thread (dyefast) in olive green, dark green and bright green, dark red, deep pink and yellow
- 6-in (15cm) embroidery ring
- Sewing machine, thread and sewing kit

Stitches
Chain stitch and French knot (see page 40), and overcast stitch (see page 44).

Preparation and cutting out
Wash and iron the linen to reduce shrinkage (see tips on page 126).

Using a photocopier, enlarge the pattern for the front and back pieces of the outer lavender sachet and the strawberry design template to full size, shown on page 45 at 75 percent. Enlarge the pattern for the inner lavender sachet to full size, also shown on page 45 but at 50 percent.

Referring to the notes on page 127, cut out one 7⅞-in (20cm) square in linen for the embroidered front of the outer sachet. This will be cut to size using the pattern after the embroidery has been completed. Cut out two back pieces in linen to pair. Cut out one piece of muslin for the inner lavender sachet.

Cottage Border Scarf

Inspired by beautiful vintage embroidery worked by my grandmother in the 1920s, this scarf has been given a modern feel by working the embroidery onto intense red wool and lining it with a contrasting vibrant green silk.

Stitches

Irregular satin stitch and satin stitch (see page 48), padded satin stitch, French knot, stem stitch and buttonhole stitch on the round (see page 49), and straight stitch (see page 123).

Preparation

Prepare the wool fabric for embroidery (see tips on page 126).

Using a photocopier, enlarge the scarf pattern to full size, shown on page 55 at 25 percent, and join the two halves together. The finished size of the template will be 60¼ x 8¼ in (153 x 21cm) including the seam allowance.

Cut out one piece of wool felt fabric for the embroidery, 64 x 12 in (163 x 12cm), which includes 2 in (5cm) extra on all sides to secure the fabric into a 6-in (15cm) embroidery ring.

Tracing the design

Working on a smooth, clean surface, place the dressmaker's carbon paper face down at one end of the wool felt fabric. Place the cottage border design template, shown on page 54 at full size, on top. Make sure it is straight and attach it with masking tape. Using a sharp pencil, carefully trace over the design, checking to make sure that it is transferring clearly (see picture 1 on page 20).

Embroidery

Place the wool felt fabric in the embroidery ring, stretching it taut and securing it firmly. Embroider the scarf exactly as described for the central group of flowers on the Cottage Border Tea Cozy (see page 48). Follow the instructions for the grass at the bottom of the design and the sunflowers, blue delphiniums and pink hollyhocks.

Press the embroidered fabric lightly on the back (see page 127).

Cutting out

Cut off the excess 2 in (5cm) round the embroidered wool so that it measures 60¼ x 8¼ in (153 x 21cm).

Cut one piece of pure silk lining in a contrasting color to 59⅞ x 8⅛ in (152 x 20.5cm) (the lining is cut slightly smaller to allow for the thickness of the wool felt to roll over the edges).

Making up the scarf

With right sides together, place the silk lining on top of the wool fabric and pin, tack and machine stitch round all the sides, leaving a 2⅜-in (6cm) gap between the balance points. Trim the corners of the scarf (see picture 1).

Turn the scarf right side out through the gap in the seam. Turn in the raw edges and close the gap with slip stitch (see picture 2; for slip stitch, see page 123).

Finishing

Carefully press all the edges of the scarf on the lining side (see notes on pressing and finishing on page 128).

Materials and equipment

- 64 x 12 in (163 x 31cm) of red wool felt (this includes and extra 2 in (5cm) to secure the embroidery ring)
- 59⅞ x 8⅛ in (152 x 20.5cm) of green silk lining
- Cottage border template (see page 54)
- Scarf pattern (see page 55)
- Dressmaker's carbon paper
- Sharp, hard pencil
- Masking tape
- 6-in (15cm) embroidery ring
- Embroidery kit and stranded cotton embroidery thread (dyefast) in dark green, bright green, orange, black, sky blue, mid pink and yellow
- Sewing machine, thread and sewing kit

cottage border scarf template

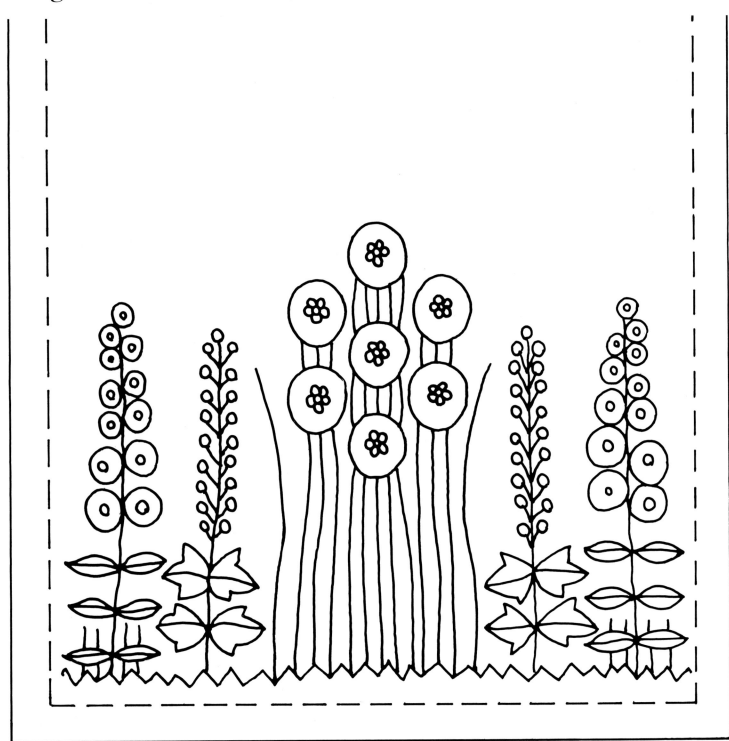

Pattern 100%

SCARF PATTERN (join the 2 halves together)
Cut 1 in wool felt after embroidery
Cut 1 in silk

Pattern 25%

Seaside

Lighthouse Beach Bag

This lighthouse design was inspired by one at the base of a headland along the bay from my cottage in Cornwall, England. Fashioned from sturdy cotton ticking, this cheerful bag is perfect for day trips to the beach.

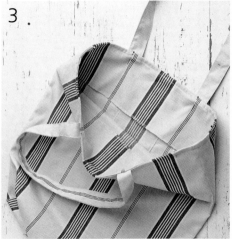

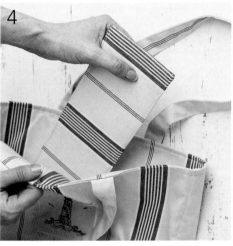

Stitches
Chain stitch (see page 126).

Preparation and cutting out
Wash and iron the cotton ticking and the linen square to reduce shrinkage (see tips on page 126).

Using a photocopier, enlarge the bag pattern with the lighthouse design template to full size, shown on page 60 at 50 percent. Enlarge the patterns for the facing, handles and cover for the base, shown on page 61 at 25 percent.

Referring to the notes on page 127, cut out all the bag pieces in the cotton ticking stripe, ensuring that the patterns are positioned on the straight grain of the fabric and follow the stripe.

Cut out the 13⅜-in (35cm) square of cream linen for the embroidered patch, making sure that you cut exactly on the straight grain of the fabric as the fraying process requires the fabric grain to be absolutely square.

Tracing the design
Working on a smooth, clean surface, place the dressmaker's carbon paper face down on the linen square and place the lighthouse design template centrally on top. Make sure it is straight on the grain of the fabric and attach it with masking tape. Using a sharp pencil, carefully trace round the lighthouse design, checking to make sure that it is transferring clearly

Materials and equipment
- ¾ yd (70cm) of cotton ticking stripe
- 7⅞ in (20cm) of iron-on interfacing
- 13⅞ x 13⅞ in (35 x 35cm) of plain cream linen for the patch
- 11⅞ x 3⅞ in (30 x 10cm) of thick cardboard for the base
- Lighthouse design template (see page 60)
- Bag pattern (see pages 60–1)
- Dressmaker's carbon paper
- Masking tape
- Sharp, hard pencil
- 10-in (25cm) embroidery ring
- Embroidery kit and stranded cotton embroidery thread (dyefast) in navy, red, blue and taupe
- Sewing machine, thread and sewing kit

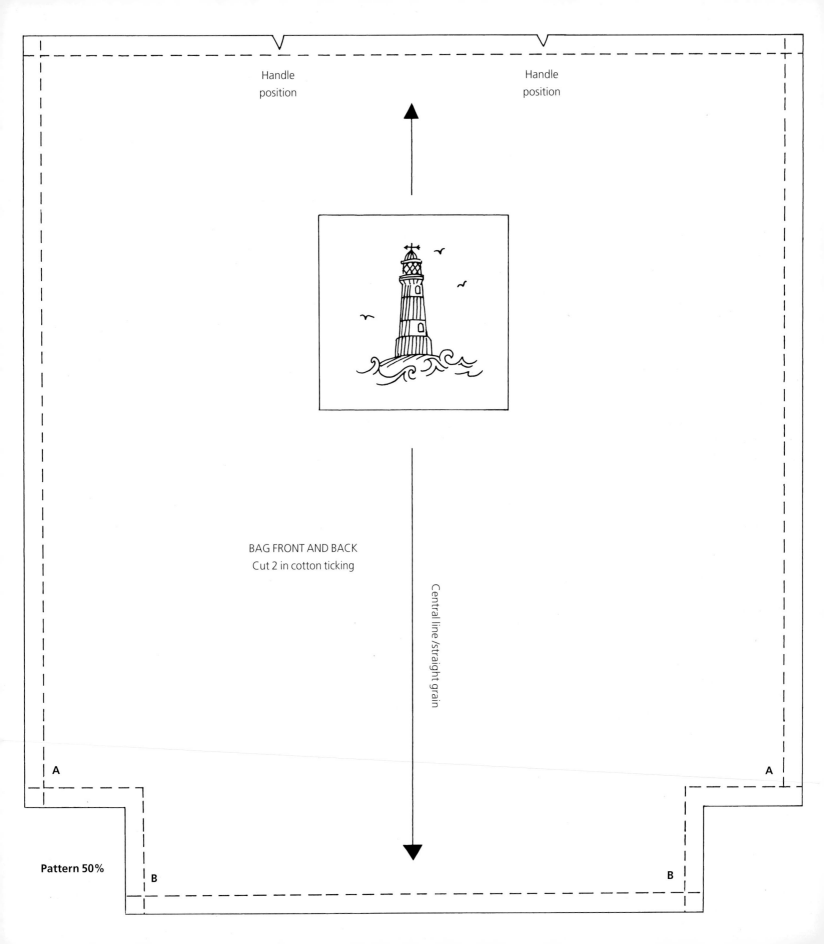

Handle
position

Handle
position

BAG FRONT AND BACK
Cut 2 in cotton ticking

Central line /straight grain

A

A

Pattern 50%

B

B

Lighthouse beach bag template

(see instructions and picture 1 for the Heart Table Runner and Napkins on page 20).

Embroidery

Secure the linen square centrally in a 10-in (25cm) embroidery ring, stretching the fabric taut. The lighthouse is embroidered using one strand of thread and fine chain stitch, as follows:

• Stitch the outline of the lighthouse and ground in navy.

• Still in navy, stitch the windows, shading, wave outlines, weather vein, lantern detail and birds.

• Work the highlights on the lighthouse dome and windows in red.

• Work the right-hand side lighthouse highlights and wave detail in blue.

• For the shading on the left-hand side of the lighthouse and the ground use taupe.

When the embroidery is complete, remove the linen fabric from the ring and press lightly on the back. Cut the square to size using the patch pattern, making sure that it is absolutely square on the straight grain of the fabric and with the embroidery in the center.

Fraying and attaching the patch

First fray the patch. Starting on one edge, pull away individual threads to produce a ½-in (1cm) fringe. Repeat the process on the other three sides (see picture 1).

Place the frayed patch on the front piece of the bag, centering it 3⅜ in (8.5cm) down from the top edge, and pin and tack it into place. Using a sewing machine, sew a very close zigzag stitch round the edges of the patch just inside the fringed edge, then machine a row of straight stitching along the inner edge of the zigzag stitch line (see picture 2). Press lightly on the reverse.

Making up the bag

Place the front and back pieces of the bag with right sides together and pin, tack and machine stitch a ½-in (1cm) seam along both

sides and along the bottom (see picture 1 on page 34). Press the seams open.

To form the gusset, with right sides together, arrange the corners of the base so that seams at point A and B match and the edges are level. Tack and machine stitch ½ in (1cm) across the corners of the base (see picture 2 on page 34). Turn the bag through to the right side.

To make the handles, place two strips with right sides together and pin, tack and machine stitch a ½-in (1cm) seam along both long edges. Turn through to the right side and press, then topstitch along both edges. Repeat to make the other handle.

Place the two facing strips with right sides together and pin, tack and machine stitch a ½-in (1cm) seam along both ends to join them together into a ring. Pin the facing to the top of the bag with right sides together, inserting the handles between the two layers of fabric at the notches. Tack and then machine stitch a ½-in (1cm) seam to join the facing and handles to the bag. Press the seams open and neaten the edges of the facing and seams with an overlocker or zigzag stitch.

Turn the facing through to the inside of the bag and press, then topstitch round the top of the bag, ½ in (1cm) in from the edge. Join the bottom of the facing to the side seams of the bag with a few slip stitches (see picture 3; for slip stitch, see page 123).

To make up the base of the bag, fold the piece of ticking in half with right sides together and pin, tack and machine stitch along the side and one end. Turn through to the right side and insert the cardboard. Turn the ends under and topstitch all the way round.

Finishing

Lightly press the bag (see notes on pressing and finishing on page 128). Then insert the base into the bag (see picture 4).

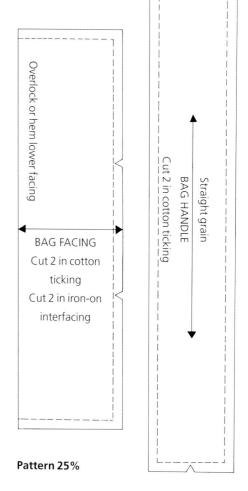

BAG FACING
Cut 2 in cotton ticking
Cut 2 in iron-on interfacing

Overlock or hem lower facing

Straight grain
BAG HANDLE
Cut 2 in cotton ticking

Pattern 25%

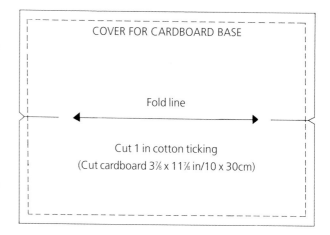

COVER FOR CARDBOARD BASE

Fold line

Cut 1 in cotton ticking
(Cut cardboard 3⅞ x 11⅞ in/10 x 30cm)

Boat Lavender Pillow

This nostalgic sailing boat bobbing on the water is a constant reminder of wonderful days spent by the sea. Filled with a separate inner sachet of fragrant lavender, it can be kept near to your bed to help relax you and induce sleep.

Materials and equipment

- 9⅞-in (25cm) length of blue and cream gingham (minimum 36 in/90cm wide)
- 13⅞ x 13⅞ in (35 x 35cm) of cream linen for patch
- 3⅞ in (10cm) of iron-on interfacing
- Four cream pompoms, 1 in (2.5cm) diameter
- 9⅞ in (25cm) of white or cream muslin for the inner lavender sachet
- 5¼ oz (170g) fragrant loose lavender
- Boat design template (see page 64)
- Pillow and inner sachet patterns (see pages 64–5)
- Sharp, hard pencil
- Dressmaker's carbon paper
- Masking tape
- 10-in (25cm) embroidery ring
- Embroidery kit and stranded cotton embroidery thread (dyefast) in brown, taupe, red, deep, light and mid blue
- Sewing machine, thread and sewing kit

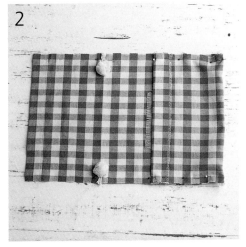

Stitches

Chain stitch and running stitch (pages 126 and 123).

Preparation and cutting out

Wash and iron the linen patch and the gingham fabric to reduce shrinkage (see tips on page 126).

Using a photocopier, enlarge the lavender pillow and inner sachet patterns to full size, shown on pages 64–5 at 37 percent. The boat design template is shown on page 65 at full size.

Referring to the notes on page 127, cut out the 13⅞-in (35cm) square of linen for the embroidered patch, making sure you cut along the straight grain of the fabric as the fraying process requires the fabric to be absolutely square. Cut out one pillow piece in gingham, ensuring that the pattern is positioned on the straight grain of the fabric and follows the lines of the check. Cut out two pieces of iron-on interfacing. Cut out one inner sachet in muslin.

boat lavender pillow template

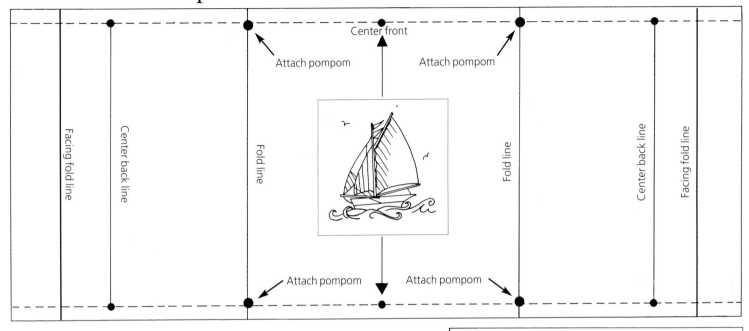

Facing fold line

Center back line

Fold line

Center front

Attach pompom · Attach pompom

Attach pompom · Attach pompom

Fold line

Center back line

Facing fold line

Pattern 37%

INTERFACING – Cut 2 in iron-on interfacing

Pattern 37%

Tracing the design

Working on a smooth, clean surface, place the dressmaker's carbon paper face down on the linen square and place the boat design template centrally on top. Make sure it is straight on the grain of the fabric and attach it with masking tape. Using a sharp pencil, carefully trace round the design, checking to make sure that it is transferring clearly (see picture 1 on page 20).

Embroidery

Secure the linen square in a 10-in (25cm) embroidery ring, positioning the design in the center and pulling the fabric taut. Work the boat embroidery as follows:
• Work the mast in chain stitch using three strands of brown.
• For the boom, work chain stitch using two strands of brown.
• Work the boat, sail and flag outline in chain stitch using one strand of deep blue.

• Shade the sails in chain stitch using one strand of taupe.
• Work the upper hull in running stitch, using six strands of light blue for the upper right-hand side and six strands of deep blue for the upper left-hand side.
• For the lower hull, work running stitch using six strands of red.
• Work the waves in chain stitch, using two strands of deep blue for the outline of the waves and two strands of mid blue for the inner waves.
• Finish by working the birds in chain stitch using one strand of deep blue.

When the embroidery is complete, remove the fabric from the ring and press lightly on the back (see page 127). Cut to size using the patch pattern, taking care that it is cut on the grain.

Fraying and attaching the patch

Fray and attach the boat patch as described for the lighthouse patch, referring to pictures 1 and 2

on page 58. Position the patch centrally on the front of the pillow, on the right side of the gingham fabric.

Once you have stitched the patch in place, press lightly on the reverse.

Making up the pillow cover

Press one piece of iron-on interfacing onto each end of the gingham on the wrong side of the fabric. Neaten the edges of the facing either by machine zigzagging or overlocking (see picture 1).

Place the gingham right side up on your work surface and tack all four pompoms into position at the marked balance points.

Turn back the facing on the right-hand side at the balance points and pin, tack and then machine stitch in place. Fold back the right side of the gingham fabric at the balance points (where the pompoms have been attached) and pin, tack and then machine stitch along the top and bottom seam lines (see picture 2).

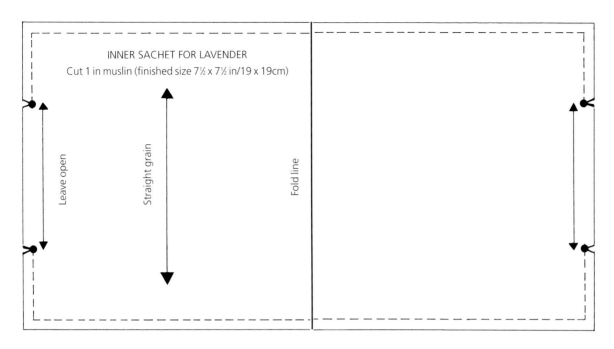

INNER SACHET FOR LAVENDER
Cut 1 in muslin (finished size 7½ x 7½ in/19 x 19cm)

Leave open

Straight grain

Fold line

Pattern 37%

Repeat this on the left side of the gingham fabric, so that it overlaps onto the right side, and pin, tack and then machine stitch along the top and bottom seam lines as before (see picture 3).

Neaten all the seams and then turn the pillow cover through to the right side, pulling out the corners where the pompoms have been attached. Press all of the edges with the tip of the iron (see notes on pressing and finishing on page 128).

Making up the inner sachet

With right sides together, sew round all the edges of the muslin, leaving a gap between the balance points. Turn the sachet through to the right side and fill it with lavender. Close the gap in the side seam with slip stitch (see page 123).

Finishing

Insert the lavender sachet into the gingham pillow cover (see picture 4).

Pattern 100%

Anchor Lavender Heart

This cute lavender heart is far too pretty to hide away in a wardrobe. Hang it from a peg, hook or doorknob for a nautical-themed decoration that will fragrance the air with relaxing lavender – perfect for a bathroom.

anchor lavender heart template

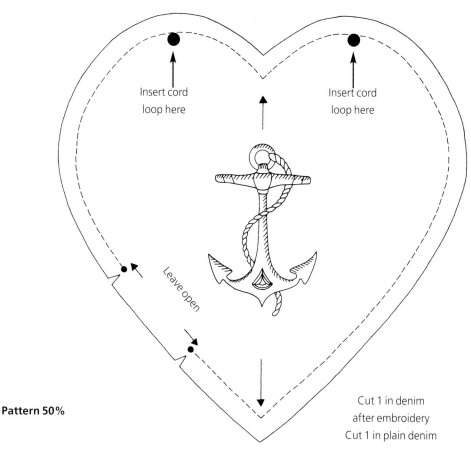

Insert cord loop here

Insert cord loop here

Leave open

Pattern 50%

Cut 1 in denim after embroidery
Cut 1 in plain denim

Stitches

Chain stitch (see page 126), satin stitch (see page 125) and straight stitch (see page 123).

Preparation and cutting out

Wash and iron the denim to reduce shrinkage (see tips on page 126). Using a photocopier, enlarge the heart pattern and anchor design template to full size, shown at 50 percent. Referring to the notes on page 127, cut out one 13⅞-in (35cm) square of denim for the embroidered front and one denim heart shape for the back.

Tracing the design

Trace the anchor design onto the center of the denim square using white dressmaker's carbon paper and a sharp pencil (see picture 1 on page 20).

Embroidery

Secure the denim square in an 8-in (20cm) embroidery ring, positioning the traced anchor design in the center. Embroider the motif as follows, using two strands of white thread throughout:

• Chain stitch the outline of the anchor and rope.

• Work the highlights on the top ring and bar in satin stitch.

• Work the side and lower highlights in straight stitch for less density of stitch.

• For the triangular area, work chain stitch.

• Fill in the inner rope with chain stitch.

When the embroidery is complete, remove

the fabric from the hoop and press lightly on the back. Cut to size using the pattern.

Making up the lavender heart

With the front piece of the heart right side up, pin then tack the ric-rac braid round the edge. Pin the hanging cord in position with the loop facing inwards, so that it will hang from the top seam when the heart is turned through (see picture 1).

Starting at the top center, machine stitch round the heart along the middle of the ric-rac braid

Materials and equipment

• 13⅞ in (35cm) of denim
• ¾ yd (70cm) of white ric-rac braid, ⅝ in (1.5cm) wide
• 15¾ in (40cm) of white silky cord, ¼ in (4mm) wide
• Anchor design template (see above)
• Heart pattern (see above)
• White dressmaker's carbon paper

• Masking tape
• Sharp, hard pencil
• 8-in (20cm) embroidery ring
• Embroidery kit and stranded cotton embroidery thread (dyefast) in white
• Sewing machine, thread and sewing kit
• 3½ oz (100g) of fragrant loose lavender

to the point at the bottom, then lift the presser foot and pivot the needle in the fabric to continue sewing round, finishing back at the top.

With right sides facing, pin, tack and machine stitch the front and back heart shapes together, using the previous stitch line as a guide. Leave a gap between the balance points on one side.

Trim the seam allowance to ⅛ in (3mm), then turn the heart right side out. Press the edges with the tip of the iron and fill with lavender. Close the gap in the side seam with slip stitch (see page 123).

Perch Cushion

This beautiful fish cushion with intricately worked stitches makes a striking accessory for a waterside home or a lovely present for fishing friends.

Materials and equipment

- 19¾ in (50cm) of cream linen (minimum 45 in/112cm wide)
- 19¾ x 19¾ in (50 x 50cm) of blue cotton (dyefast) for the contrasting piping
- 2¼ yds (2m) of cotton piping cord, ⅛ in (3mm) wide
- 3⅞ in (10cm) of iron-on interfacing
- 2 flat cream buttons, 1 in (2.5cm) diameter
- Perch design template (see page 71)
- Cushion pattern (see pages 70–1)
- Sharp, hard pencil
- Dressmaker's carbon paper
- Masking tape
- 12-in (30cm) embroidery ring
- Embroidery kit and stranded cotton embroidery thread (dyefast) in deep blue, mid blue and white
- Sewing machine, thread and sewing kit
- 15 x 11⅞ in (38 x 30cm) feather-filled cushion inner

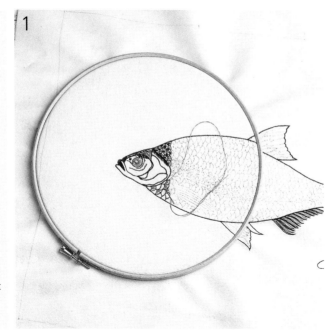

1

2

3

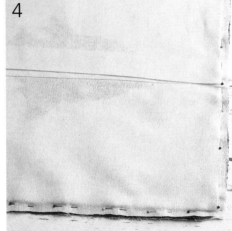

4

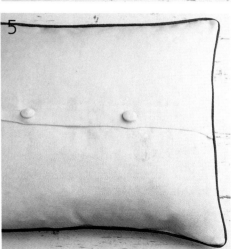

5

Stitches

Chain stitch (page 126), straight stitch (page 123), satin stitch (page 125) and French knot (page 124).

Preparation and cutting out

Wash and iron the linen (see tips on page 126).

Using a photocopier, enlarge the perch design template and cushion pattern to full size, shown on pages 70–1 at 40 percent. Referring to the notes on page 127, cut out one front piece in linen with an extra 2 in (5cm) all round to secure the embroidery ring, two back pieces in linen, two pieces of linen, 19⅛ x 1¼ in (48.5 x 3cm), for the interfacing, and a total of 79 in (2m) of strips of bias-grain cotton for the piping (see pictures 2 and 3 on page 25 for how to prepare bias strips for piping).

Tracing the design

Trace the perch design onto the center of the linen front piece. Working on a smooth, clean surface, place dressmaker's carbon paper face down on the fabric and tape the template on top, making sure it is straight on the grain of the fabric. Using a sharp pencil, carefully trace round the design, checking to make sure that it is transferring clearly (see picture 1 on page 20).

Embroidery

Secure the linen in a 12-in (30cm) embroidery ring with the design in the center; move it along as you work (see picture 1). Embroider as follows:

- Work the fish outline and the head contours in chain stitch using two strands of deep blue.
- For the head detail, work chain stitch using one strand of deep blue. Fill in the solid areas with satin stitch using three strands of deep blue.
- For the eye, make a central French knot using three strands of white. Work straight stitch round the knot using two strands of white for the upper left of the eye and two strands of mid blue for the rest.

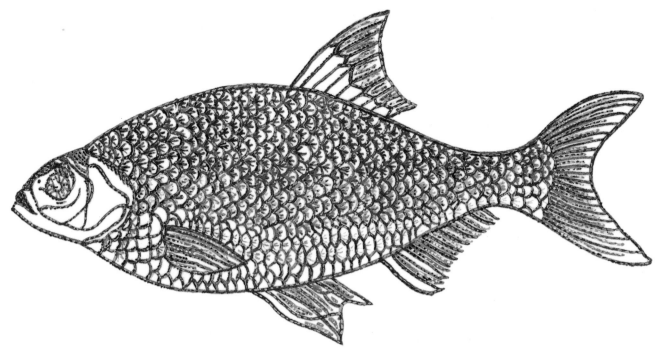

• Chain stitch the main lines of the fins and tail using one strand of deep blue.

• Outline the scales with chain stitch using one strand of deep blue. Fill them in with straight stitch using three strands of deep blue for the upper body, mid blue for the middle body and white for the lower body.

When the embroidery is complete, remove the fabric from the ring and press the back (see page 127). Cut to size using the front pattern piece.

Making up the cushion

For the piping, fold the bias strip of contrasting cotton in half over the piping cord and pin, tack

and machine stitch close to the cord (see picture 2). Pin, tack and machine stitch the piping all round the edge of the front piece of the cushion, with the embroidered side facing up, easing the piping round the corners. When you reach the place where you started, cut the inner cord so that the ends butt together and firmly overstitch. Trim the

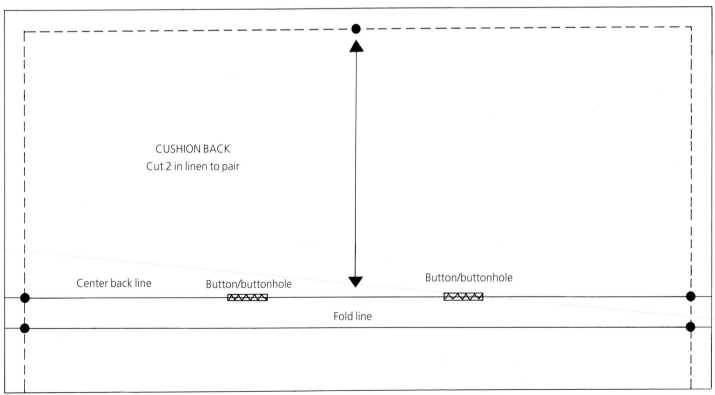

CUSHION BACK
Cut 2 in linen to pair

Center back line

Button/buttonhole

Button/buttonhole

Fold line

Pattern 40%

perch cushion template

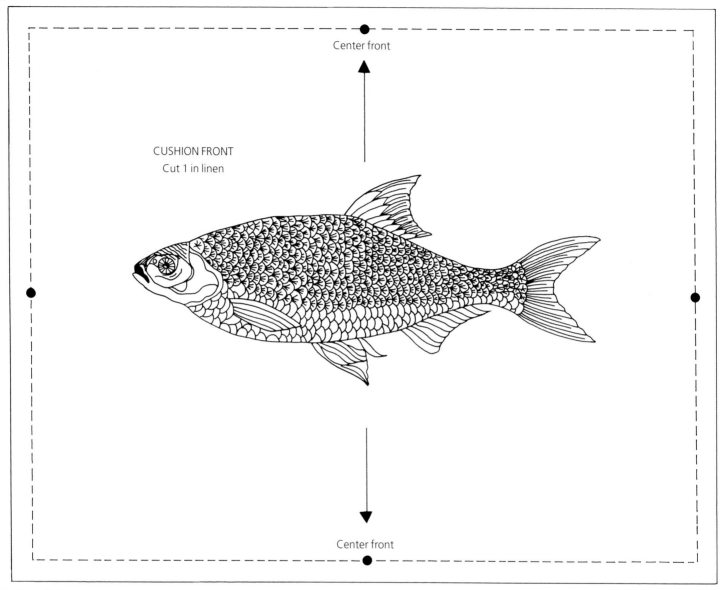

Center front

CUSHION FRONT
Cut 1 in linen

Center front

Pattern 40%

piping fabric so that the ends overlap each other and turn one end under by ½ in (1cm). Tuck the other raw end underneath it and stitch (see picture 3).

Press iron-on interfacing onto the back of each facing section on the back cushion pieces. Fold under and press a hem of ¼ in (5mm) on the outer edge. Fold back the facing sections at the balance points so that wrong sides are together and press. Pin, tack and machine the facing in place with a row of stitching 1 in (2.5cm) from the edge.

Mark the buttonhole positions on the top back piece and work two ⅞-in (2cm) buttonholes by machine. Sew two buttons into positions at the marked points on the lower back piece.

With the center back balance points matching at the sides, place the top back cushion piece over the bottom back cushion piece and pin in place. Tack and machine stitch to secure. With right sides together, pin, tack and then machine stitch the front and back cushion pieces together,

following the previous stitch line done for the piping and pivoting the needle at the corners to allow for the bulk of the piping (see picture 4).

Trim the corners to reduce the bulk and neaten the raw edges. Turn the cushion cover through to the right side and pull out the corners.

Finishing
Lightly press the edges with the tip of the iron and insert the inner cushion pad (see picture 5).

Shell Toiletry Bag

This exquisite drawstring bag is embroidered with a row of three shells in classical style. The neutral colors draw attention to the shapes and textures, while the white facings emphasize the raised ridges of the shells.

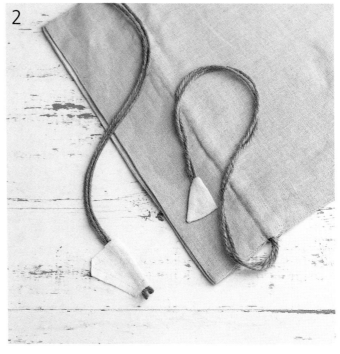

Stitches

Padded satin stitch and satin stitch (see page 125), and chain stitch (see page 126).

Preparation and cutting out

Wash and iron the fabric (see tips on page 126).

Using a photocopier, enlarge the shells design template and bag, facing and tie end patterns to full size, shown on pages 74–5 at 50 percent.

Referring to the notes on page 127, cut out the following: one bag front in natural linen, with an extra 2 in (5cm) at the bottom and sides to secure the fabric into an embroidery ring, one bag back in natural linen, two bag facings in white linen and two decorative ends for the rope ties in white linen.

Tracing the design

Working on a smooth, clean surface, place dressmaker's carbon paper face down on the right side of the bag front piece and place the shells design template centrally on top, 1¼ in (3cm) up from the bottom edge. Make sure the template is straight on the grain of the fabric and attach it with masking tape. Using a sharp pencil, carefully trace round the design, checking to make sure that it is transferring clearly (see picture 1 on page 20).

Embroidery

Secure the fabric in a 12-in (30cm) embroidery ring, positioning the shells design in the middle. Work the embroidery as follows:
- Left shell (Gastropod):

Stitch the outline and main contours in padded satin stitch using two strands of white.

For the shading on each side of the shell and on the inner shell, work fine chain stitch using one strand of taupe.

For the shell markings, follow the lines with satin stitch using two strands of beige.
- Middle shell (Cockle):

Chain stitch the outline using two strands of white.

Work the highlights of the ridges in padded satin stitch using two strands of white, starting at the bottom and tapering towards the top.

Add a line of chain stitch to outline the shaded area using two strands of beige. For the shading, work fine chain stitch with one strand of taupe.

For the horizontal shell markings, work a fine line of chain stitch using one strand of beige.
- Right shell (Volute):

Stitch the outline and the main contours in padded satin stitch using two strands of white.

For the shaded areas, work fine chain stitch using one strand of taupe.

Materials and equipment

- 19¾ in (50cm) of natural linen (min 36 in/90cm wide)
- 5⅞ in (15cm) of contrasting white linen for the facings and decorative tie ends
- 3⅓ yds (3m) of natural rope/cord, ¼ in (4mm) wide
- Shells design template (see page 74)
- Bag pattern (see pages 74–5)
- Sharp, hard pencil
- Dressmaker's carbon paper
- Masking tape
- 12-in (30cm) embroidery ring
- Embroidery kit and stranded cotton embroidery thread (dyefast) in white, taupe and beige
- Sewing machine, thread and sewing kit
- 2-in (5cm) safety pin to thread the rope or cord

shell toiletry bag template

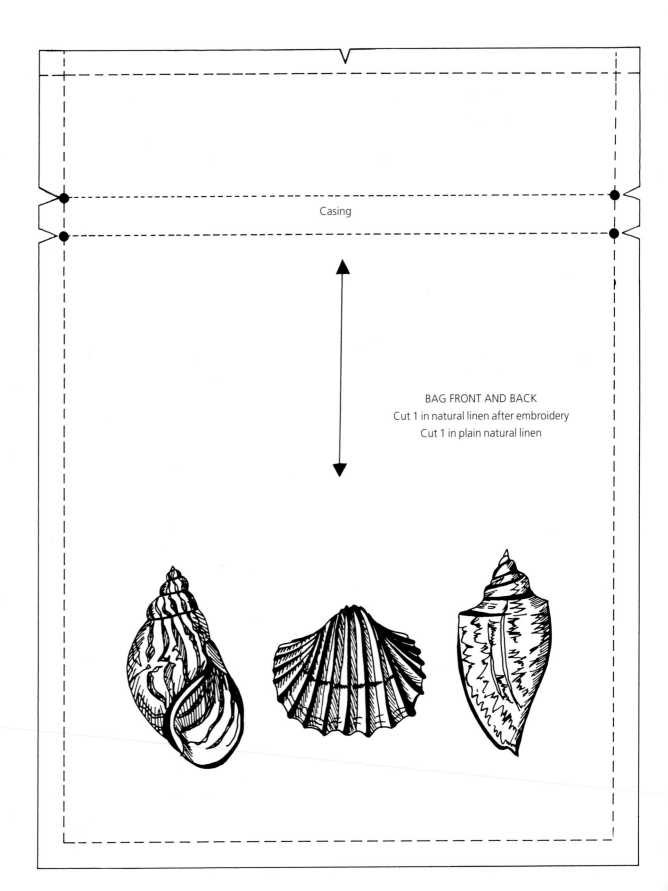

Casing

BAG FRONT AND BACK
Cut 1 in natural linen after embroidery
Cut 1 in plain natural linen

Pattern 50%

For the inner detail, work fine chain stitch using one strand of beige.

When the embroidery is complete, remove the linen from the ring and press lightly on the back (see page 127). Cut the bag front to size using the front dolly bag pattern.

Making up the bag

With right sides together, join the front and back bag pieces together by pinning, tacking and machine stitching a ½-in (1cm) seam all round the sides and bottom, starting and finishing at the lower set of balance points. Turn the fabric through to the right side and press.

To prepare the channel for the drawstrings, work on the front and back sections of the bag separately. With right sides together, pin, tack and machine stitch the front and back facings onto the front and back of the bag with a ½-in (1cm) seam all round, stitching from the upper set of balance points to form the frill.

Trim the corners and turn the frill through to the right side. To form the channel, fold and press under a ½-in (1cm) hem on the facing and pin, then tack it to the bag. Machine stitch along the bottom edge of the facing, then machine stitch a parallel row ⅞-in (2cm) above the first row of stitching (see picture 1).

Press and stitch round the edge of the top and sides of the frill for a crisp finish.

Lay the bag flat and at the point where the upper row of stitching forms the channel, on each side, join the front and back together by firmly overstitching by hand.

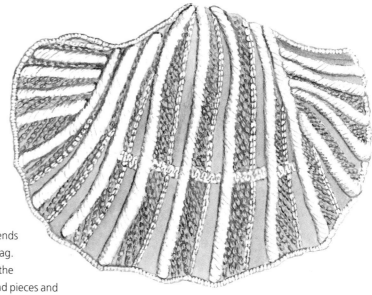

Using a safety pin, thread one piece of rope or cord right through the front and back of the drawstring channel so that the two ends meet at one side of the bag. Place the two ends onto the decorative white linen end pieces and stitch as shown, continuing down the small side seam. Turn the decorative linen ends through to the right side, fold the raw edges inside, press and stitch the edges to finish. Repeat with the other piece of rope or cord, threading it through the opposite side of the casing and attaching the second white tie end (see picture 2).

Finishing

Pull both pieces of rope or cord at opposite sides of the casing so that the top of the bag draws in, closing the bag and forming the handles by which to hang up the bag.

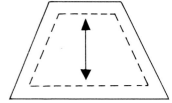

DECORATIVE TIE END
Cut 2 in white linen

Pattern 50%

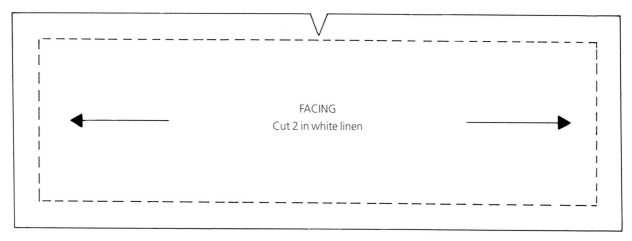

FACING
Cut 2 in white linen

Pattern 50%

Botanicals and Bugs

Lavender Pillow

For centuries, lavender has been cultivated not only for its horticultural beauty and its aroma, but also for its properties of relaxation – it can help to encourage sleep when placed beside your pillow. Traditionally, lavender sachets were used to keep linens smelling fresh and to protect woollens from moths. This design is stitched with tiny chain stitch, straight stitch and French knots onto cream linen.

Stitches

Chain stitch (see page 126), straight stitch (see page 123) and French knot (see page 124).

Preparation and cutting out

Wash and iron the linen and gingham fabric to reduce shrinkage (see tips on page 126).

Using a photocopier, enlarge the lavender pillow pattern to full size, shown on page 80 at 50 percent. The lavender design template is shown on page 80 at full size. Referring to the notes on page 127, cut out one 13⅞-in (35cm) linen square for the embroidered front and cut out one gingham square for the back piece using the pattern.

Tracing the design

Working on a smooth, clean surface, place the dressmaker's carbon paper face down in the center of the linen square. Place the lavender design template on top, making sure it is straight on the grain of the fabric, and secure it with masking tape. Using a sharp pencil, carefully trace round the design, checking to make sure that it is transferring clearly (see picture 1 on page 20).

Embroidery

Secure the linen square in a 6-in (15cm) or 8-in (20cm) embroidery ring with the traced lavender design in the center, making sure the fabric is stretched taut. Work the embroidery as follows:

• Chain stitch the outline of the stems using one strand of sage green.

• Work all the leaves and the veins in chain stitch using one strand of olive green.

• Chain stitch the lavender buds using one strand of purple.

• Fill in the buds with straight stitch using six strands of lavender.

• Work French knots at the tips of the lavender buds using six strands of purple.

• Finish the edges of the square with French knots using six strands of purple.

When the embroidery is complete, remove the fabric from the hoop, wash if necessary and press lightly on the back (see notes on page 127). Cut the linen to size using the front pattern piece.

Making up the lavender sachet

Place the embroidered front and the gingham back with right sides together and pin, tack and machine stitch round the edges, leaving a gap between the balance points (see picture 1).

Trim the corners to reduce bulk, turn the sachet right side out and press lightly round the edges with the tip of the iron.

Fill the sachet with lavender using a teaspoon (see picture 2) and then close the opening with slip stitch (see page 123).

Finishing

Make a knot about 1 in (2.5cm) from both ends of the ribbon. Stitch the knots onto the front of the linen square, ½ in (1cm) in from each side. Machine-stitch round the very outer edge of the square.

Materials and equipment

• 13⅞-in (35cm) square of cream linen for the front
• 6¾-in (17cm) square of purple and white gingham for the back
• 15¾ in (40cm) of cream satin ribbon, ⅜ in (7mm) wide
• Lavender design template and lavender pillow pattern (see page 80)
• Dressmaker's carbon paper
• Sharp, hard pencil
• Masking tape
• 6-in (15cm) or 8-in (20cm) embroidery ring
• Embroidery kit and stranded cotton embroidery thread (dyefast) in sage green, olive green, purple and lavender
• Sewing machine, thread and sewing kit
• 3½ oz (100g) of fragrant loose lavender
• Teaspoon to insert lavender

lavender pillow template

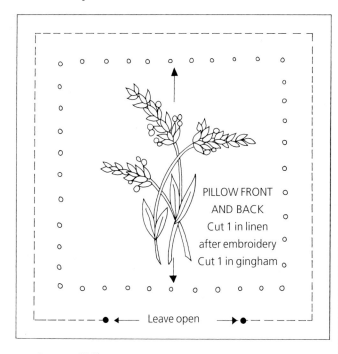

PILLOW FRONT
AND BACK
Cut 1 in linen
after embroidery
Cut 1 in gingham

← Leave open →

Pattern 50%

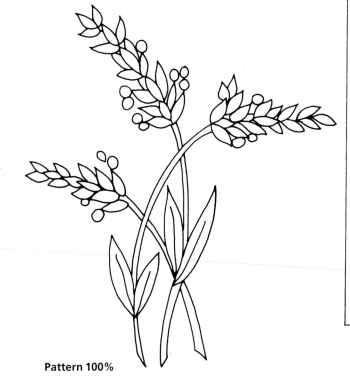

Pattern 100%

lavender cushion template

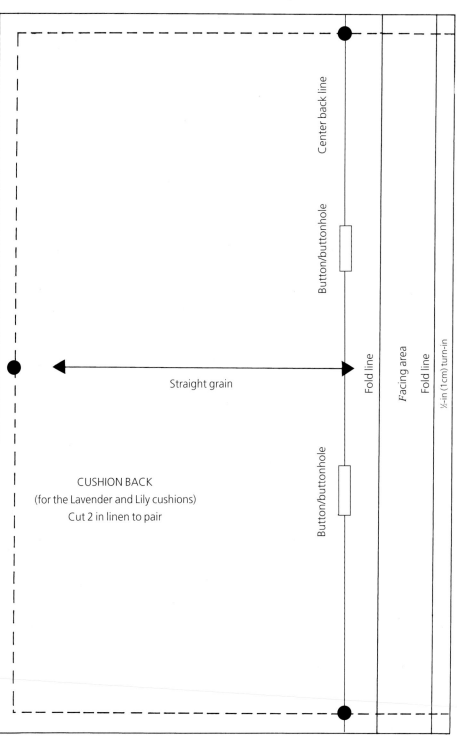

Center back line

Button/buttonhole

Fold line

Facing area

Fold line

½-in (1cm) turn-in

Straight grain

Button/buttonhole

CUSHION BACK
(for the Lavender and Lily cushions)
Cut 2 in linen to pair

lavender cushion template

CUSHION FRONT
Cut 1 in linen

Piped edges

Straight grain

Pattern 50%

Lavender Cushion

With its wonderful pungent aroma, this cushion reminds me of the old stable where I store sacks of loose lavender for the sachets I make. It's a favorite old-fashioned scent that brings back memories of past summers and the beautiful sight of intense blue lavender fields.

Stitches

Chain stitch (see page 126), straight stitch (see page 123) and French knot (see page 124).

Preparation and cutting out

Wash and iron the linen to reduce shrinkage (see tips on page 126).

Using a photocopier, enlarge the cushion pattern and lavender design template to full size, shown on pages 80–1 at 50 percent.

Referring to the notes on page 127, cut out one front cushion piece in linen, with an extra 2 in (5cm) all round to allow the fabric to be secured into the embroidery ring. Cut out two back cushion pieces in linen. Cut out two pieces of iron-on interfacing, 19⅛ x 1¼ in (48.5 x 3cm). Following the instructions on pages 25–6, cut out a total of 79 in (2m) of bias strips in green cotton for the contrasting piping.

Tracing the design

Working on a smooth, clean surface, place the dressmaker's carbon paper face down in the center of the linen square. Place the lavender design template on top, making sure it is straight on the grain of the fabric, and secure it with masking tape. Using a sharp pencil, carefully trace round the design, checking to make sure that it is transferring clearly (see picture 1 on page 20).

Embroidery

Secure the linen square in a 12-in (30cm) embroidery ring, positioning the traced lavender design in the center and stretching the fabric taut. Move the ring across the fabric as necessary as you work. Work the central lavender design first and then the lavender border, as follows:

• Chain stitch the outline of the lower stems (1 in/2.5cm) using one strand of khaki green.
• Chain stitch the outline of the upper stems and those forming the border round the design using one strand of sage green.
• Work all the leaves and the veins in chain stitch using one strand of olive green.
• Chain stitch the outline of the lavender buds using one strand of purple.
• Fill in the buds with straight stitch using six strands of lavender.
• Finish with French knots at the tips of the lavender buds using six strands of purple.

When the embroidery is complete, remove the fabric from the ring, wash if necessary and press lightly on the back (see notes on page 127).

Cut the linen to size using the pattern for the front piece of the cushion.

Making up the cushion

Make the contrasting insertion piping and then pin, tack and machine stitch it round all the edges of the front piece of the cushion (see instructions for the Perch Cushion on pages 69–71).

Press iron-on interfacing onto the back of each facing section on the back cushion pieces. Fold under and press a hem of ½ in (1cm) on the outer edge. Fold back the facing sections at the balance points so that wrong sides are together and press. Pin, tack and machine stitch the facing in place with a row of stitching 1 in (2.5cm) from the edge.

Mark the buttonhole positions along the center back line on the upper back piece and work two buttonholes by machine. Sew two buttons into position at the marked points on the upper edge of the lower back piece.

With the center back balance points matching on both sides, place the upper back piece of the cushion over the lower back piece, fasten the buttons and pin and tack in place.

With right sides together, join the front and back cushion pieces. Pin, tack and machine stitch in place, following the stitch line done for the piping and pivoting the needle at the corners to allow for the bulk of the piping.

Finishing

Trim the corners to reduce bulk and neaten the raw edges. Turn the cushion cover through to the right side and pull out the corners. Lightly press all the edges with the tip of the iron. Insert the inner cushion pad.

Materials and equipment

- 19¾ in (50cm) of cream linen (min 45 in/112cm wide)
- 19¾-in (50cm) square of green cotton (dyefast) for the contrasting insertion piping
- 2¼ yds (2m) of piping cord, ⅛ in (3mm) wide
- 3⅞ in (10cm) of iron-on interfacing
- 2 flat cream buttons, 1 in (2.5cm) diameter
- Lavender design template (see page 81)
- Cushion pattern (see pages 80–1)
- Dressmaker's carbon paper
- Sharp, hard pencil
- Masking tape
- Metal ruler
- 12-in (30cm) embroidery ring
- Embroidery kit and stranded cotton embroidery thread (dyefast) in khaki green, sage green, olive green, purple and lavender
- Sewing machine, thread and sewing kit
- 15 x 15 in (38 x 38cm) cushion inner

Lily Cushion

The classic white lily, my favorite formal flower, stands majestic and sublime. It is worked with tiny chain stitches in a combination of greens, pale gray and taupe.

Stitches

Chain stitch (see page 126), bullion knot (see page 87) and straight stitch (see page 123).

Preparation and cutting out

Wash and iron the linen to reduce shrinkage (see tips on page 126).

Using a photocopier, enlarge the lily design template and front cushion pattern to full size, shown on page 86 at 50 percent. Enlarge the back cushion pattern to full size, shown on page 80 at 50 percent. Referring to the notes on page 127, cut out one front piece in linen, with an extra 2 in (5cm) all round to secure the embroidery ring. Cut out two back pieces in linen. Cut out two pieces of iron-on interfacing, 19⅛ x 1¼ in (48.5 x 3cm).

Following the instructions on pages 25–6, cut out a total of 79 in (2m) of bias strips in green cotton for the contrasting piping.

Tracing the design

Working on a smooth, clean surface, place the dressmaker's carbon paper face down in the center of the linen square. Place the lily design template on top, making sure it is straight on the grain of the fabric, and secure it with masking tape. Using a sharp pencil, carefully trace round the design, checking to make sure that it is transferring clearly (see picture 1 on page 20).

Embroidery

Secure the linen square in a 12-in (30cm) embroidery ring, positioning the traced lily design in the center and stretching the fabric taut. Move the ring across the fabric as necessary as you work. Work all of the lily embroidery in fine chain stitch except for the inner stamen, which are worked in bullion knots, as follows:

• Stitch the outline of the lily stems and leaves using two strands of dark green.
• Work the main contours of the stems and leaves using one strand of dark green.
• Work the highlights on the upper part of the leaves using one strand of fresh green.
• Stitch the inner section of the leaves using one strand of taupe.
• Work further stitch lines in sage and olive green, following the contours on the leaves and using one strand of thread.
• Stitch the outline of the lily head using two strands of silver gray.
• Work the main contours of the lily head using one strand of silver gray.
• For the shaded areas of the lilies and contour lines, use one strand of taupe.
• Outline the stamens using one strand of thread, first in silver gray then with an inner line in yellow.
• Work the center of the stamen with a bullion knot using six strands of orange.
• Outline the long stamen stem using one strand of silver gray.
• Stitch the long stamen stem with one strand of dark green and follow round the outline to the tip and back again to form two rows on the stem.
• Fill in the long stamen ends with straight stitch using two strands of taupe.

When the embroidery is complete, remove the fabric from the hoop, wash if necessary and press the back (see notes on page 127). Cut the linen to size using the front pattern piece.

Making up the cushion

Make the contrasting insertion piping and then pin, tack and machine stitch it round all the edges of the front piece of the cushion (see instructions for the Perch Cushion on pages 69–71).

Press iron-on interfacing onto the back of each facing section on the back cushion pieces. Fold under and press a hem of ½ in (1cm) on the outer edge. Fold back the facing sections at the balance points so that wrong sides are together and press.

Materials and equipment

- 19⅞ in (50cm) of cream linen (minimum 45 in/112cm wide)
- 19⅞-in (50cm) square of green cotton (dyefast) for the contrasting insertion piping
- 2¼ yds (2m) of piping cord, ⅛ in (3mm) wide
- 3⅞ in (10cm) of iron-on interfacing
- 2 flat cream buttons, 1 in (2.5cm) diameter
- Lily design template (see page 86)
- Front cushion pattern (see page 86) and back cushion pattern (see page 80)
- Dressmaker's carbon paper
- Sharp, hard pencil
- Masking tape
- Metal ruler
- 12-in (30cm) embroidery ring
- Embroidery kit and stranded cotton embroidery thread (dyefast) in dark green, fresh green, taupe, sage green, olive green, silver gray, yellow and orange
- Sewing machine, thread and sewing kit
- 15 x 15 in (38 x 38cm) feather-filled cushion inner

Stem Rose Cushion Pad

The rose is a perennial favorite and traditionally the flower of love. It is sewn with tiny chain stitches and patched into the middle of this country-style cushion.

Materials and equipment

- 9⅞-in (25cm) square of cream linen
- 19¾ in (50cm) of cream and green gingham
- Approximately 39½ in (1m) of pompom insertion braid
- Stem rose design template (see page 90)
- Cushion pattern (see pages 90–1)
- Dressmaker's carbon paper
- Sharp, hard pencil
- Masking tape
- 6-in (15cm) embroidery ring
- Embroidery kit and stranded cotton embroidery thread (dyefast) in deep green, light green, deep pink and light pink
- Sewing machine, thread and sewing kit
- 15¾ in (40cm) of 4 oz wadding for the cushion inner

Stitches

Chain stitch (see page 126).

Preparation and cutting out

Wash and iron the linen and gingham fabrics to reduce shrinkage (see tips on page 126).

Using a photocopier, enlarge the cushion pattern to full size, shown on page 91 at 25 percent. The central patch with the stem rose design template is shown on page 90 at full size. Trim the pattern to fit your chair seat by tracing round the base. Check that it is the same on both sides, then add a ½-in (1cm) seam allowance all round.

Referring to the notes on page 127, cut out one 9⅞-in (25cm) square of linen for the embroidered

section. Cut out the top and bottom strips for the front of the cushion cover in gingham. Cut out two side patches on the cross grain in gingham for the front of the cover. Cut out four ties in gingham. Cut out one back piece in gingham, using your own seat pattern. Finally, cut two pieces of wadding, using your own seat pattern but without the ½-in (1cm) seam allowance.

Tracing the design

Working on a smooth, clean surface, place dressmaker's carbon paper face down on the linen square and tape the stem rose design template on top, making sure it is centered and straight on the grain of the fabric. Using a sharp

pencil, trace round the design, checking to make sure that it is transferring clearly (see page 20).

Embroidery

Secure the linen square in an 6-in (15cm) embroidery ring, positioning the traced stem rose design in the center and stretching the fabric taut. Move the ring across the fabric as necessary as you work. The stem rose is embroidered entirely in chain stitch as follows:

- Outline the left side of the stem using one strand of deep green.
- Stitch the right side of the stem using two strands of light green.
- Outline the main leaves and the small rose

stem rose template

leaves using one strand of deep green.
• Work the upper leaf veins using one strand of
deep green and the lower leaf veins using one
strand of light green.
• Fill in the small rose leaves using one strand of
deep green.
• Stitch the outline of the rose head using one
strand of deep pink.
• Fill the shaded areas using one strand of deep pink.
• Complete the rose head by filling in the
remaining areas using one strand of light pink.
    When the embroidery is complete, remove the
linen from the ring, wash if necessary and press
lightly on the back (see page 127). Cut the fabric
to size using the central patch pattern piece.

Making up the cushion

With right sides together, pin, tack and machine
stitch one of the gingham patches that has been
cut out on the cross grain onto one side of the
embroidered patch, taking care not to stretch the
gingham. Repeat to attach the other gingham
patch onto the other side of the embroidered
patch. Press the seams open (see picture 1).
    With right sides together, pin, tack and machine
stitch one of the gingham strips to the top edge
of the three joined patches. Then join the bottom
gingham strip in the same way to form the front
cover of the cushion. Press the seams open. Using
your chair-seat pattern, cut the front piece to size.
    Fold the four ties down the center with right
sides facing and stitch down the length of each
one, ½ in (1cm) in from the edge. Turn the ties
right side out, using a safety pin to ease the fabric
through, and iron them flat. Attach the ties by
pinning, tacking and machine stitching them in
place between the balance points (see picture 2).
    Pin, tack and machine stitch the pompom
insertion braid round the front and sides of the
back piece of the cushion, starting and finishing
at the ties. Attach the braid to the right side of
the fabric with the pompoms facing inwards.
    With right sides facing, pin the front and back
pieces of the cushion cover together with the

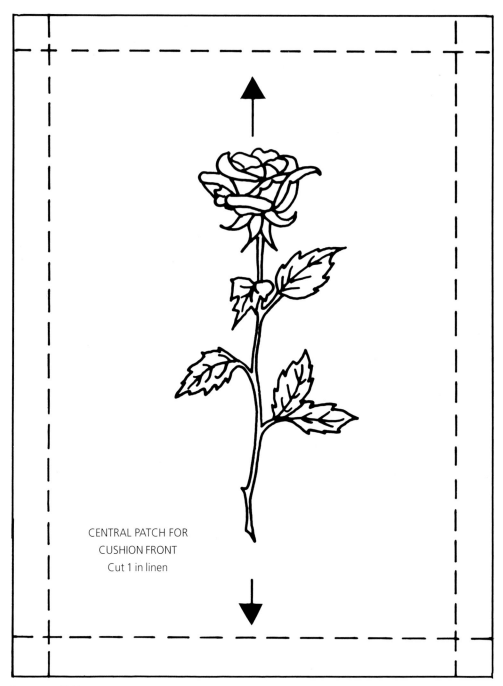

CENTRAL PATCH FOR
CUSHION FRONT
Cut 1 in linen

Pattern 100%

pompom braid sandwiched between (see picture
3). Tack and machine stitch in place, following the
previous stitch line done for the pompom braid
and easing the needle at the curved corners to
allow for the bulk of the braid. Leave a gap of
about 5⅞ in (15cm) in the back seam between
the ties to turn the cushion cover through.

Finishing

Trim the corners to reduce bulk and neaten the
raw edges. Turn the cushion cover through and
pull out the corners. Press the edges with the
tip of the iron. Insert the inner wadding pieces
through the gap in the back seam (see picture 4)
and then close it with slip stitch (see page 123).

stem rose cushion pad template

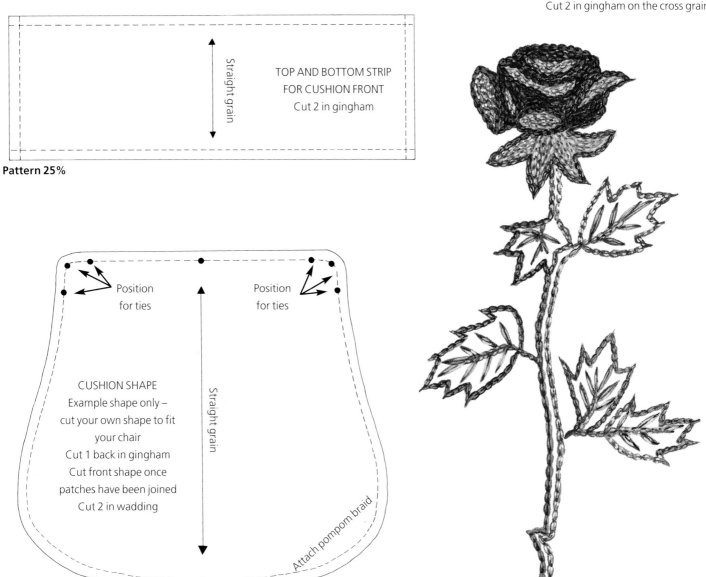

Straight grain and fold line

TIES FOR CUSHION PAD – Cut 4 in gingham

Pattern 25%

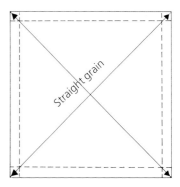

Straight grain

Pattern 25%

SIDE PATCH FOR CUSHION FRONT
Cut 2 in gingham on the cross grain

Straight grain

TOP AND BOTTOM STRIP
FOR CUSHION FRONT
Cut 2 in gingham

Pattern 25%

Position
for ties

Position
for ties

Straight grain

CUSHION SHAPE
Example shape only –
cut your own shape to fit
your chair
Cut 1 back in gingham
Cut front shape once
patches have been joined
Cut 2 in wadding

Attach pompom braid

Pattern 25%

Bee Cushion and Lavender Heart

Embroidered with tiny chain stitches and French knots, this little black bee, embellished with stripes of antique gold, was inspired by a mural I once painted in the Belvoir carriage on the Orient Express.

Stitches

Chain stitch (see page 126) and French knot (see page 124).

Preparation and cutting out

Wash and iron the linen to reduce shrinkage (see tips on page 126).

Using a photocopier, enlarge the front cushion pattern to full size, shown below at 25 percent. Enlarge the back cushion pattern to full size, shown on page 94 at 25 percent. The bee design template is shown on page 94 at full size.

Referring to the notes on page 127, cut out one cushion front piece in linen, with an extra 2 in (5cm) all round to secure the embroidery ring. Cut out two cushion back pieces in linen. Cut out two pieces of iron-on interfacing, 19⅛ x 1¼ in (48.5 x 3cm). Following the instructions on pages 25–6, cut out a total of 79 in (2m) of bias strips in black cotton for the insertion piping.

Materials and equipment

- 19¾ in (50cm) of cream linen (minimum 45 in/112cm wide)
- 19¾-in (50cm) square of black cotton (dyefast) for the insertion piping
- 2¼ yds (2m) of cotton piping cord, ⅛ in (3mm) wide
- 3⅞ in (10cm) of iron-on interfacing
- 2 flat cream buttons, 1 in (2.5cm) diameter
- Bee design template (see page 94)
- Front cushion pattern (see right) and back cushion pattern (see page 94)
- Dressmaker's carbon paper
- Sharp, hard pencil
- Masking tape
- 12-in (30cm) embroidery ring
- Embroidery kit and stranded cotton embroidery thread (dyefast) in black and antique gold
- Sewing machine, thread and sewing kit
- 15 x 15 in (38 x 38cm) feather-filled cushion inner

Tracing the design

Using the cushion front pattern, mark the positions of the bees on the front piece of the cushion. Working on a smooth, clean surface, place dressmaker's carbon paper face down on the front of the linen square and tape the bee design template in position on top, making sure it is straight on the grain of the fabric. Using a sharp pencil, carefully trace round the design, checking to make sure that it is transferring clearly (see picture 1 on page 20). Repeat for all nine bees.

Embroidery

Secure the linen square in a 12-in (30cm) embroidery ring, positioning the first traced bee design in the center and stretching the fabric taut. Move the ring across the fabric as necessary as you work. Embroider each bee as follows:

- Chain stitch the outline of the body and the wings using one strand of black.
- Work the antennae, legs and wing detail in chain stitch using one strand of black.
- For the black striped body area, work across with

bee cushion template

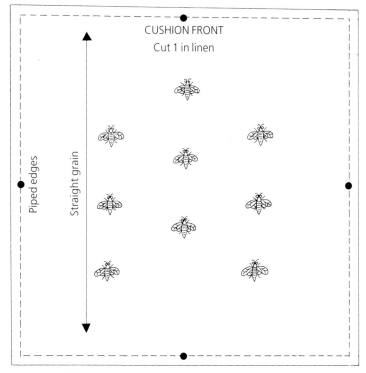

CUSHION FRONT
Cut 1 in linen

Piped edges

Straight grain

Pattern 25%

bee cushion template

CUSHION BACK
Cut 2 in linen to pair

Straight grain

Button/buttonhole   Button/buttonhole

Fold line
Facing area
Fold line
½-in (1cm) turn-in

Pattern 25%

lavender heart template

Attach loop
in seam

FRONT AND BACK
Cut 1 in linen after
embroidery
Cut 1 in plain linen

Straight grain

Leave open

Pattern 50%

two or three rows of chain stitch using one strand.
• Fill between the black stripes with antique gold,
working across with one or two rows of chain
stitch using one strand.
• Finish with two French knots for the eyes, using
four strands of black.

When the embroidery is complete, remove the
fabric from the ring, wash if necessary and press
the back (see notes on page 127). Cut the linen
to size using the cushion front pattern.

Making up the cushion

Make the contrasting insertion piping and then
pin, tack and machine stitch it round all the edges
of the front piece of the cushion (see instructions
for the Perch Cushion on pages 69–71).

Press iron-on interfacing onto the back of each
facing section on the back cushion pieces. Fold
under and press a hem of ½ in (1cm) on the outer
edge. Fold back the facing sections at the balance
points so that wrong sides are together and press.
Pin, tack and machine stitch the facing in place
with a row of stitching 1 in (2.5cm) from the edge.

Mark the buttonhole positions along the center
back line on the upper back piece of the cushion
and work two buttonholes by machine. Sew two

buttons into position at the marked points on
the lower back piece of the cushion.

With the center back balance points matching
on both sides, place the upper back piece of the
cushion over the top edge of the lower back piece,
fasten the buttons and pin and tack in place.

With right sides together, join the front and
back cushion pieces. Pin, tack and machine stitch
in place, following the stitch line done for the
piping and pivoting the needle at the corners to
allow for the bulk of the piping.

Finishing

Trim the corners to reduce
bulk and neaten the
raw edges. Turn
the cushion cover
through to the right
side and pull out
the corners. Lightly
press the edges
with the tip of
the iron and
then insert
the inner
cushion pad.

BEE DESIGN
As used on the
cushion and
lavender heart.
The eyes are 2
French knots

Pattern 100%

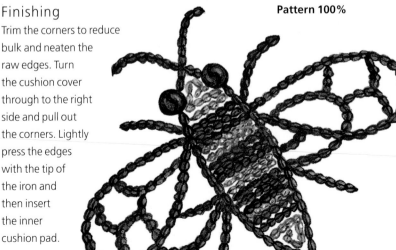

Lavender Heart

Stitches

Chain stitch (see page 126) and French knot (see page 124).

Preparation and cutting out

Wash and iron the linen to reduce shrinkage (see tips on page 126).

Using a photocopier, enlarge the heart pattern to full size, shown opposite at 50 percent. The bee design template is shown opposite at full size.

Referring to the notes on page 127, cut out one 9⅞-in (25cm) square in linen for the embroidery to be worked for the front of the heart. Cut out one heart shape for the back using the pattern.

Tracing the design

Working on a smooth, clean surface, place dressmaker's carbon paper face down on the front of the linen square and tape the bee design template on top, making sure it is centered and straight on the grain of the fabric. Using a sharp pencil, trace round the design, checking to make sure that it is transferring clearly (see page 20).

Embroidery

Secure the linen square in a 6-in (15cm) embroidery ring, positioning the traced bee design in the center. Work the embroidery for the bee as described on pages 93–4.

When the embroidery is complete, remove the fabric from the ring and press lightly on the back. Cut out the heart shape using the pattern, making sure the embroidered bee is in the center.

Making up the lavender heart

Fold the black satin ribbon in half to form a loop and pin then tack it into position on the right side of the front piece of the heart, with the loop facing inwards so that it will hang from the top seam when it is turned through.

With right sides facing, pin, tack and machine stitch the front and back pieces of the heart

together, leaving a gap between the balance points to turn it through (see picture 1).

Clip the curved edges to give a better shape (see picture 2). Turn the fabric through to the right side and press the edges of the heart with the tip of the iron to define its shape.

Finishing

Fold the muslin ribbon in half to find the center and sew it in position at the top of the heart. Tie the ribbon into a bow.

Use a teaspoon to fill the heart with lavender. Then close the gap with slip stitch (see page 123).

Materials and equipment

- 9⅞ in (25cm) of cream linen
- 9⅞ in (25cm) of black satin ribbon for loop, ¼ in (5mm) wide
- 19¾ in (50cm) of black muslin ribbon for bow, 1 in (2.5cm) wide
- Bee design template (see opposite)
- Lavender heart pattern (see opposite)
- Sharp, hard pencil
- Masking tape
- Dressmaker's carbon paper
- 6-in (15cm) embroidery ring
- Embroidery kit and stranded cotton embroidery thread (dyefast) in black and antique gold
- Sewing machine, thread and sewing kit
- 2½ oz (70g) of fragrant loose lavender

Dragonfly Picture

Based on a design for a silk bolero inspired by the 1920s' Ballet Rousses, this dragonfly, in shades of blue, has a luminous quality with its fragile wings joined together by tiny gossamer silver threads.

Stitches

Chain stitch and zigzag chain stitch (see page 126), satin stitch (see page 125) and straight stitch (see page 123).

Preparation and cutting out

Wash and iron the linen to reduce shrinkage (see tips on page 126).

Using a photocopier, enlarge the dragonfly design template to full size, shown on page 99 at 45 percent. Referring to the notes on page 127, cut out one 17¾-in (45cm) square in linen.

Tracing the design

Working on a smooth, clean surface, place dressmaker's carbon paper face down on the front of the linen square and tape the dragonfly design template on top, making sure it is centered and straight on the grain of the fabric. Using a sharp pencil, carefully trace round the design, checking to make sure that it is transferring clearly (see picture 1 on page 20).

Embroidery

Secure the fabric in a 12-in (30cm) embroidery ring, positioning the traced dragonfly design in the center and stretching the fabric taut. Move the ring across the fabric as necessary as you work. Embroider the dragonfly as follows:
• Work the outline of the dragonfly's body, head, legs and wings in chain stitch using one strand of deep blue.
• Continue the deep blue line in chain stitch to form the tail.

• Repeat the outline with a parallel inner stitch line in soft blue.
• For the legs, fill in between the deep blue outline with one row of chain stitch using one strand of soft blue.
• Stitch the inner long part of the body with a repeated pattern, working from the top to the bottom using one strand of thread as follows: chain stitch diagonal lines in soft blue, horizontal lines in deep blue followed by soft blue and then deep blue. Fill in the triangular shapes with satin stitch using two strands of silver lurex thread.
• Chain stitch the wide middle body area to create a crisscross detail using one strand of soft blue.
• Fill in between the crisscrossed areas with chain stitch using one strand of silver.
• For the upper body, satin stitch the sections using two strands of deep blue and fill in the gaps with satin stitch using two strands of silver.
• For the head, chain stitch two parallel rows, each using one strand of deep and soft blue to form the chevron shape.
• Outline the eye and nose detail with chain stitch using one strand of deep blue, then infill horizontally with satin stitch using two strands of silver.
• Work the two remaining head sections in vertical satin stitch using two strands of silver.
• For the upper wings (nearest to the head), first chain stitch the four long horizontal lines using one strand of soft blue.
• Fill in between these lines with small vertical straight stitches about ⅛ in (3mm) apart using four strands of silver.

Materials and equipment

• 17¾-in (45cm) square of cream or white linen
• Dragonfly design template (see page 99)
• Dressmaker's carbon paper
• Sharp, hard pencil
• Masking tape
• 12-in (30cm) embroidery ring
• Embroidery kit and stranded cotton embroidery thread (dyefast) in deep blue, soft blue, silver lurex and lavender
• Pins
• Iron and wide padded board
• Simple, light-colored frame, 12–15 in (30–38cm) square (or larger if using a mount within the frame)

- Work the lavender-colored long, undulating lines of chain stitch using one strand.
- Join up these lines with a mix of zigzag chain stitch with gaps of about ¼ in (4mm) using two strands of silver, and straight stitch using four strands of silver. Work until the wing veins are joined together throughout with small silver stitches.
- Work the lower wings in chain stitch, using one strand of soft blue for the outer lines and one strand of lavender for the inner lines.
- As on the upper wings, work a mix of straight stitch and zigzag chain stitch using silver thread until the wing veins are joined up throughout.

When the embroidery is complete, remove the fabric from the hoop, wash if necessary and press lightly on the back (see notes on page 127).

Framing the embroidery

For best results, have the embroidery framed professionally, so that it is properly stretched before it is mounted.

To do it yourself, dampen the fabric with clean water. Remove most of the moisture by laying it flat and then folding or rolling it up in a towel for 15 minutes. Remove the towel and lay the fabric embroidered side down on a wide padded board and pin each corner in place. Working methodically, pin the straight edges in place, first in the center, gently stretching the cloth so that it is equally taut all round, and adding pins along the edges as you go. Dry the fabric gently using a warm to hot iron. When completely dry, remove the pins and secure the piece in your chosen frame.

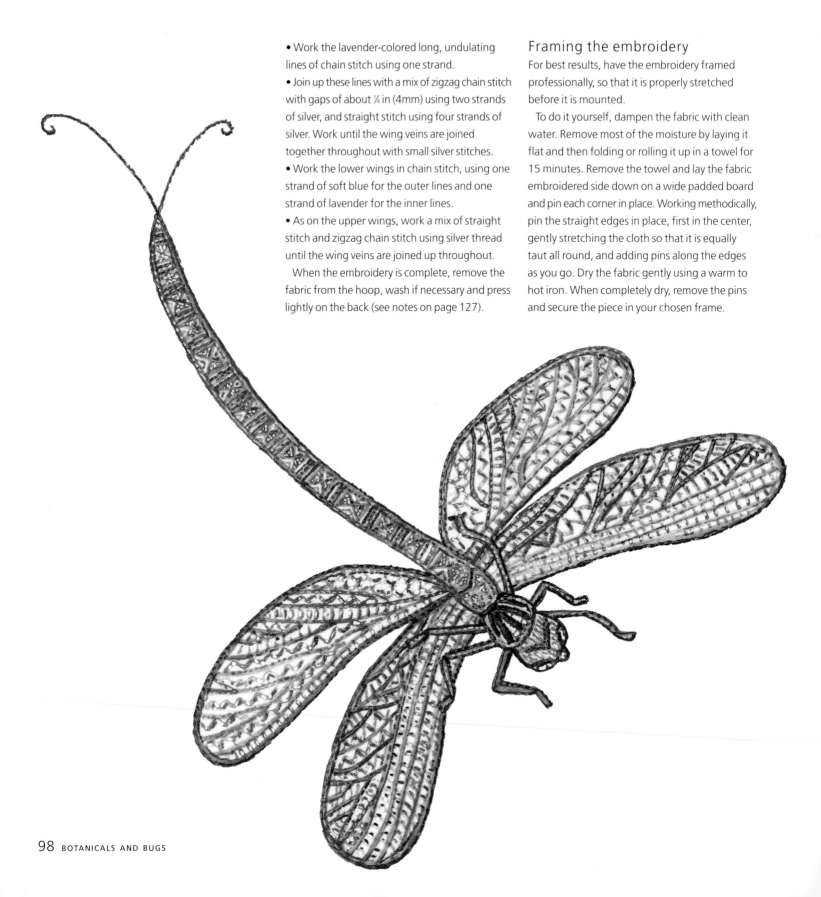

Straight grain

Cut 1 in linen
(Finished size 17¾ x 17¾ in/45 x 45cm)

Pattern 45%

Celebrations

Snowflake Hearts

These decorative hearts are embroidered with a traditional snowflake design and can be filled with lavender, spices or rose petals. They make a lovely addition to my Christmas keepsakes and look wonderful hung in a window.

Stitches

Chain stitch and zigzag chain stitch (see page 126), French knot (see page 124) and blanket stitch (see page 122).

Preparation and cutting out

The snowflake design template and heart pattern are shown on pages 104–5 at full size.

Referring to the notes on page 127, cut out one 11⅞-in (30cm) square of wool for the front embroidery. Using the pattern, cut out two back pieces in wool to make up the heart shape.

Tracing the design

Working on a smooth, clean surface, place dressmaker's carbon paper face down on the front of the wool square and tape the snowflake design template centrally on top, straight on the grain of the fabric. Using a sharp pencil, trace round the design, checking to make sure that it is transferring clearly (see picture 1 on page 20).

Embroidery

Secure the wool square in an 8-in (20cm) embroidery ring, positioning the traced snowflake design in the center. Embroider the snowflake motif using white or deep red thread throughout to contrast with the wool fabric, as follows:
• Work the outline of the snowflake in chain stitch using two strands.
• For the inner detail, work zigzag chain stitch using two strands.
• Finish with French knots using six strands.

When the snowflake embroidery is complete, remove the fabric from the ring and press lightly on the back (see notes on page 127). Cut the front piece to size using the heart pattern.

Making up the lavender heart

With right sides facing, pin, tack and machine stitch the two back pieces of the heart together, leaving a gap between the two balance points. Press the seam open (see picture 1).

Materials and equipment
- 11⅞ in (30cm) of wool felt in red or cream
- 15¾ in (40cm) of red silky cord, ¼ in (4mm) wide, or cream ribbon, ⅜ in (7mm) wide
- Snowflake design template (see page 105)
- Heart pattern (see pages 104–5)
- Sharp, hard pencil
- Dressmaker's carbon paper
- Masking tape
- 8-in (20cm) embroidery ring
- Embroidery kit and stranded cotton embroidery thread (dyefast) in red or cream to contrast with the wool
- Sewing machine, thread and sewing kit
- 3oz (80g) of fragrant loose lavender, rose petals or Christmas spice
- Teaspoon to insert the scented filling

snowflake heart template

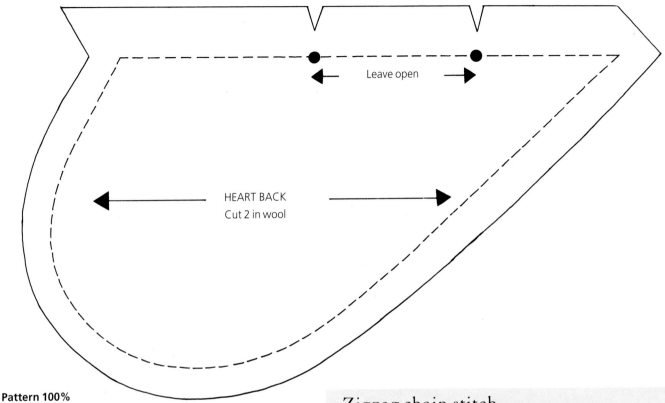

Leave open

HEART BACK
Cut 2 in wool

Pattern 100%

If using a cord hanging loop, place it in position at the balance points so that it will hang from the top seam once the heart has been stitched together. Pin the front and back pieces of the hearts together with wrong sides facing. Starting at the top center of the heart, tack and then machine stitch round the edge of the heart with a ½-in (1cm) seam allowance. Machine another stitch line on the outer edge, running parallel to the previous stitch line.

Finishing

Starting at the center top, work blanket stitch round the edge of the heart using six strands of contrasting thread, following the inner machined hemline as a guide and spacing the stitches ⅜ in (8mm) apart (see picture 2).

If using ribbon to hang the heart rather than cord, fold it in half and cross one end over the other by 2 in (5cm). Sew it to the top center of the heart by machine or by hand.

Using a teaspoon, fill the heart with lavender, rose petals or Christmas spice and close the gap with slip stitch (see page 123).

Zigzag chain stitch

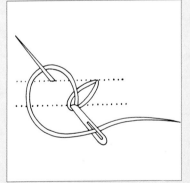
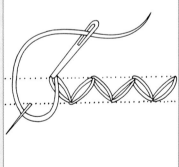

This is a type of chain stitch and is worked between two parallel marked lines.

Bring the needle to the front of the fabric and then put the needle back in at the same place. Bring the needle back out a little to the left on the opposite line, forming the loop by keeping the working thread under the tip of the needle. Put the needle back in again and then bring it out on the opposite line, a little to the left, forming the loop again. Repeat as required.

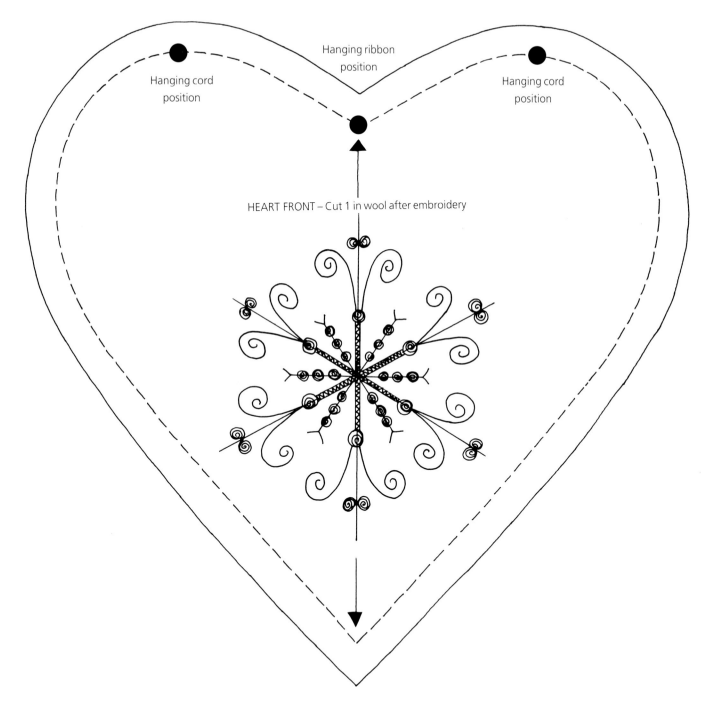

Hanging ribbon
position

Hanging cord
position

Hanging cord
position

HEART FRONT – Cut 1 in wool after embroidery

Pattern 100%

Star and Stripe Cushion

These simple contemporary cushions are easy to make with cross-stitched appliquéd stripes topped with a single star. They make a striking present and add a colorful statement to any room.

Stitches

Blanket stitch (see page 122) and cross stitch (see page 108).

Preparation and cutting out

Prepare the wool fabric by pressing (see page 126).

Using a photocopier, enlarge the patterns for the cushion, star and stripes to full size, shown on pages 108–9 at 37 percent.

Referring to the notes on page 127, cut out one cushion front piece and two cushion back pieces in red wool. Cut out two back facings in red cotton and two in iron-on interfacing.

Appliqué embroidery

Referring to the instructions for using bonding web on pages 11–12, trace the design for the appliqué stripes onto a piece of bonding web using a sharp pencil. Iron the bonding web onto the wrong side of the cream wool fabric. Trace the design for the star onto another piece of bonding web and iron the bonding web onto the wrong side of the blue wool fabric.

Cut out the stripes and star neatly on the inside of the lines and peel the bonding web backing off. Pin the three cream stripes onto the front piece of the cushion, matching the balance points (see picture 1). Press the back of the red fabric to fuse them into position.

Place the blue star in the center of the cushion, as shown on the pattern. Using a cloth to protect the wool, press the star on from the front.

Using six strands of thread, work the appliqué embroidery as follows (see picture 2):

Materials and equipment

- 15¾ in (40cm) of red wool felt (minimum 52 in/130cm wide)
- 5⅞ in (15cm) of cream wool felt (minimum 45 in/110cm wide) for the appliqué stripes
- 7⅞-in (20cm) square of blue wool felt for the appliqué star
- 3⅞ in (10cm) of red cotton for the back facings
- 3⅞ in (10cm) of iron-on interfacing
- 29⅜ in (75cm) of bonding web
- Sharp, hard pencil
- 2 buttons, ⅞ in (2cm) diameter
- Star and stripe design templates (see page 109)
- Cushion pattern (see pages 108–9)
- Sewing machine, thread and sewing kit
- Embroidery kit and stranded cotton embroidery thread (dyefast) in red and cream
- Ironing cloth
- 13⅜ x 19¾ in (34 x 50cm) feather-filled cushion inner

• Using red thread, work cross stitch neatly along each side of the three stripes, sewing all the diagonal stitches first one way and then back the other way to complete the rows.

• Work blanket stitch in cream thread round the outline of the star, with ¼-in-long (5mm) stitches spaced ⅛ in (4mm) apart.

Making up the cushion

Press iron-on interfacing onto the wrong side of each of the cotton back facings. With right sides together, pin, tack and machine one facing and one cushion back piece together along what will be the opening edge of the cushion back. Fold back the facing onto the wrong side of the back piece, turning under a ½-in (1cm) hem along the facing edge. Pin, tack and machine stitch this into place. Do the same on the opposite cushion back piece. Press for a neat finish.

Mark the two buttonhole positions on the hemmed edge of the left back piece, as marked on the pattern, then work 1-in (2.5cm) buttonholes by machine or by hand.

Overlap the left back piece over the right back piece, matching the center back balance points at the top and bottom. Sew two buttons in place in the corresponding positions on the hemmed edge of the right back piece. Do up the buttons and tack into position at the top and bottom.

With wrong sides together, join the front and back pieces of the cushion cover by pinning, tacking and machine stitching a ½-in (1cm) seam round all four sides. Machine a parallel row along the outer edge.

Finishing

Work blanket stitch round the edges of the cushion using six strands of cream thread, neatly following the inner machine hemline as a guide and spacing each stitch ½ in (1cm) apart.

Lightly press the cushion cover (see notes on pressing and finishing on page 128) and then insert the inner cushion pad.

Pattern 37%

Cross stitch

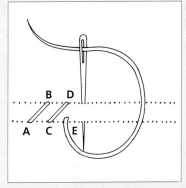
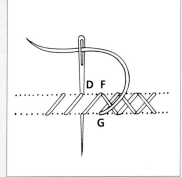

Cross stitch is one of the oldest and best-known embroidery stitches. It is quick to do and very effective, as long as the stitches all run in the same direction and are the same size.

Mark two parallel lines on the fabric. Bring the needle to the front of the fabric at point A. Put the needle in at point B and bring it out again at point C. Then put the needle in again at point D and bring it out at point E, continuing to the end of the row.

For the top row of stitches that complete the crosses, use the same holes and work back. Bring the needle out on the bottom row at point G and put it in at point D. Continue in this way to finish the row.

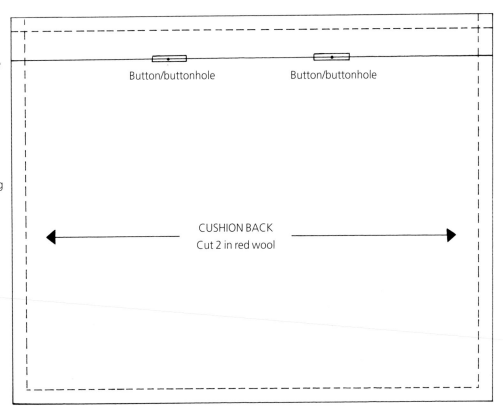

Button/buttonhole   Button/buttonhole

CUSHION BACK
Cut 2 in red wool

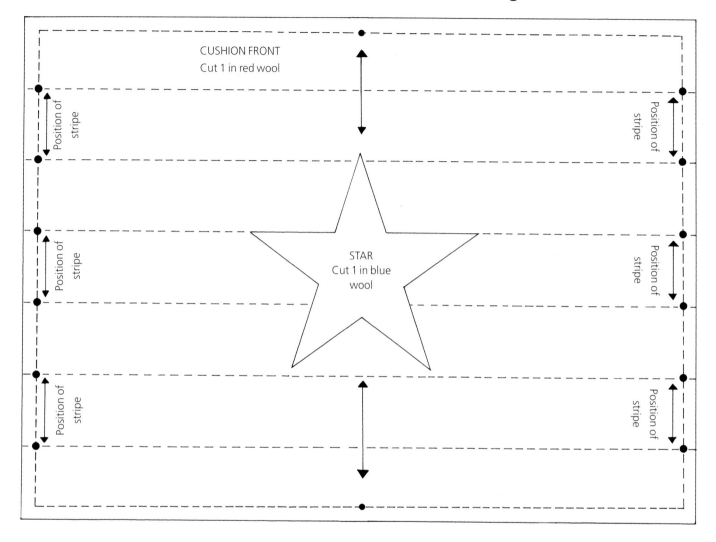

Pattern 37%

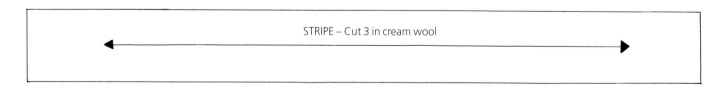

STRIPE – Cut 3 in cream wool

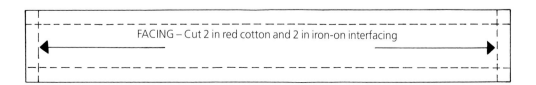

FACING – Cut 2 in red cotton and 2 in iron-on interfacing

Pattern 37%

Berry Wreath Throw

Vivid and dramatic in black wool, this throw is inspired by traditional patchwork quilts. The wreath is a striking example of appliqué embroidery, with stylized leaves and berries that lend themselves perfectly to this technique.

Stitches

Stem stitch, chain stitch, blanket stitch appliqué and blanket stitch edging (see page 113).

Preparation and cutting out

Prepare the wool fabric by pressing it (see tips on page 126).

Using a photocopier, enlarge the central wreath design template and the corner heart motif to full size, both shown on page 112 at 50 percent.

Referring to the notes on page 127, cut out the throw in black wool felt, 63 x 51¼ in (160 x 130cm).

Tracing the design

Working on a smooth, clean surface, place dressmaker's carbon paper face down in the center of the front of the wool square and tape the wreath design template on top, making sure it is straight on the grain of the fabric. Using a sharp pencil, trace round the design, checking to make sure that it is transferring clearly (see picture 1 on page 20). You will need to follow the outline to work the initial stem stitch, which holds the design together, and to guide the placement of the appliqué berries and leaves.

Appliqué embroidery

Trace the wreath design onto two pieces of bonding web, following the instructions for using bonding web on pages 11–12. Note that when the design is not symmetrical, as here, the tracing paper needs to be turned over to trace the design through, as the final motif will appear the opposite way round on the fabric. Trace four heart motifs onto a third piece of bonding web.

Iron one piece of bonding web with the traced wreath design onto the wrong sides of one red wool square and iron the other onto the wrong side of the green wool square. Cut out the berries in the red fabric and the leaves in the green fabric, cutting neatly on the inside of the line. Peel the bonding web backing off and pin all the pieces right side up on the traced design on the front of the throw. Iron to fuse the fabrics together, using a cloth to protect the wool and prevent the hot iron from making it shiny.

Iron the third piece of bonding web with the heart designs onto the second red wool square.

It is not essential to use an embroidery ring for appliqué work, but it helps when there is finer detail involved, as in this design. Position the wreath in the center of a 12-in (30cm) embroidery ring, moving it along the fabric as you work as necessary. Work the embroidery as follows:

• Work the heart outline of the central wreath in stem stitch using six strands of deep green to create a line ⅛ in (3mm) wide.
• Work the berry stems in chain stitch using three strands of deep green.
• Appliqué the leaves with blanket stitch using three strands of light green, working stitches ¼ in (4mm) long and spacing them ¼ in (4mm) apart.
• Appliqué the berries with blanket stitch using three strands of red, working stitches as above.
• Appliqué the four red corner hearts with blanket stitch using six strands of black, working stitches approximately ¼ in (6mm) long and spacing them ¼ in (6mm) apart.

Making up the throw

Tack and then machine stitch a neat ½-in (1cm) hem all round the throw. Machine another parallel line of stitching on the very edge of the blanket.

Work blanket stitch round the edge of the throw using six strands of red thread, following the inner hemline and spacing the stitches ¼ in (1cm) apart.

Materials and equipment

- 1¾ yds (160cm) of black wool felt (minimum 52 in/130cm wide) for the throw
- Two 12-in (30cm) squares of red wool felt for the appliqué berries and hearts
- 8-in (20cm) square of light green wool felt for the appliqué leaves
- Approximately 12 x 16 in (30 x 40cm) of bonding web
- Wreath and heart design templates (see page 112)
- Dressmaker's carbon paper
- Masking tape
- Sharp, hard pencil
- 12-in (30cm) embroidery ring
- Embroidery kit and stranded cotton embroidery thread (dyefast) in deep green, light green, red and black
- Sewing machine, thread and sewing kit
- Ironing cloth

Finishing

Press the throw lightly using a damp cloth to protect the fabric from the iron (see page 128).

berry wreath template

BERRY WREATH THROW
Position the traced design and heart motifs as in the diagram above. Final throw size 63 x 51¼ in (160 x 130cm).

Pattern 50%

Pattern 50%

Stem stitch

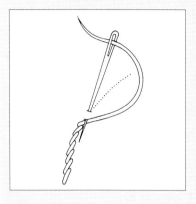

Working from left to right, bring the needle out to the front of the fabric and, slanting a little, put the needle in to the right and bring it back out halfway along the working stitch. Continue as required.

Chain stitch

One of the oldest and most widely used stitches, chain stitch is used as an outline or a filling stitch by working multiple rows.

Work the chain downwards, making a series of loops the same size and not too tight or they will lose their shape. Bring the needle out to the front of the fabric and return it through the same point, bringing it out again to cover the working thread with the needle, forming a loop. Repeat as required and finish the last loop with a tiny straight stitch.

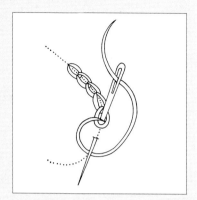

Blanket stitch appliqué

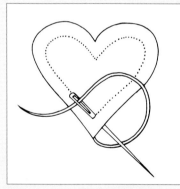
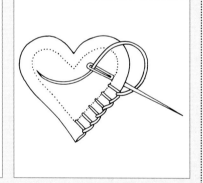

With the heart shape securely in place, mark an inner stitch guideline and work from left to right. Bring the needle to the front of the main fabric, just below the lower point of the heart. Put the needle into the heart on the upper marked line, one space to the right and straight out again, just below the front edge, over the top of the working thread. Continue as required, spacing the stitches evenly along the row so that they are symmetrical on both sides of the heart.

Blanket stitch edging

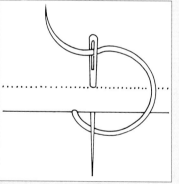
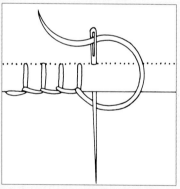

Mark a stitch guideline parallel to the edge. Working from left to right, bring the needle out to the front of the fabric very close to the edge. Put the needle in on the upper line, one space to the right, and bring it through to the front again over the top of the working thread. Continue as required, spacing the stitches evenly along the row. To finish, secure the thread by making a tiny stitch on the edge.

Reindeer
and Dove Cushions

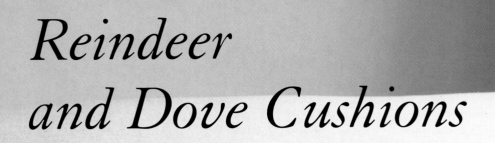

The design for the majestic and graceful reindeer was based on a pair of
beautiful bronzes that belonged to my great-grandmother. As I embroidered
the dove, the bird of peace, I thought about our world. This is a cushion
embroidered with a message, as with so many of my designs.

Stitches

For the reindeer: blanket stitch appliqué and blanket stitch edging (see page 122), zigzag chain stitch and chain stitch (see page 126), and satin stitch (see page 125).

For the dove: stem stitch (see page 123), blanket stitch appliqué and blanket stitch edging (see page 122), and French knot (see page 124).

Preparation and cutting out

Prepare the wool fabric by pressing (see page 126).

Using a photocopier, enlarge the reindeer or dove design template to full size, shown on pages 116 and 117 at 50 percent. Enlarge the cushion pattern to full size, shown on pages 32–3 at 50 percent.

Referring to the notes on page 127, cut out one front and two back pieces in red wool. Cut out two back facings in cotton and two in iron-on interfacing.

Appliqué embroidery

Referring to the instructions on pages 11–12, trace the reindeer or dove design onto bonding web with a sharp pencil. Trace the leaves for the dove cushion onto another piece of bonding web. Note that when the design is not symmetrical, as here, the tracing paper needs to be turned over to trace the design through, or the motif will appear the opposite way round on the cushion.

Iron the bonding web with the reindeer or dove design onto the wrong side of the cream wool felt. Iron the bonding web with the mistletoe design onto the wrong side of the green wool felt. Cut out the shapes neatly on the inside of the lines and peel the bonding web backing off.

Pin the felt shapes in place right side up on the front piece of the cushion. Press to fuse the fabrics together, using a cloth to protect the wool.

Position the appliqué in the middle of a 12-in (30cm) embroidery ring, moving it along as you work. It is not essential to use a hoop for appliqué embroidery, but it helps when there is fine detail.

Reindeer cushion

Work all the embroidery in red thread as follows:
• For the base or rock, sew blanket stitch ¼ in (4mm) long, spaced ⅛ in (3mm) apart, using four strands.

• Work blanket stitch round the outline of the body of the reindeer using six strands.
• Outline the antlers, head and hooves in zigzag chain stitch using two strands.
• Chain stitch the detail on the eye, nose and mouth using two strands.
• Fill in the solid area of the nose with satin stitch using three strands.
• Work blanket stitch round the edges of the cream appliquéd corner hearts using six strands, working stitches approximately ¼ in (6mm) long and spacing them ¼ in (6mm) apart.

Dove cushion

• Work the branch in stem stitch using six strands of green, tapering slightly ¼ in (4mm) towards the end.
• Blanket stitch neatly round the outline of the dove using four strands of red, working stitches ¼ in (4mm) long and spacing them ¼ in (4mm) apart.
• Appliqué the leaves with blanket stitch using three strands of light green, working stitches ¼ in (4mm) long and spacing them ¼ in (4mm) apart.
• Appliqué the berries with blanket stitch using three strands of red, working stitches ⅛ in (3mm) long and spacing them evenly on the round.
• For the eye, make a French knot using six strands of red.
• Blanket stitch the edges of the cream appliquéd hearts using six strands of red, working stitches ¼ in (6mm) long and spacing them ¼ in (6mm) apart.

Making up

The cushion is made up in the same way as the Heart Cushion (see pages 14–15).

Press iron-on interfacing onto the wrong side of the cotton back facing. Turn the outer edge under by ½ in (1cm) and press the hem in place.

With right sides together, pin, tack and machine stitch the facing to one of the back cushion pieces, sewing a ½-in (1cm) seam. Press the seam open, then fold back onto the wrong side of the cushion and press. Pin, tack and machine a line 1⅜ in (3.5cm) from the edge to hold the facing in place. Machine two parallel lines, one on the edge and the other ½ in (1cm) from the edge. Repeat for the opposite back cushion piece and facing.

Mark two buttonhole positions on the wrong side of the upper cushion back piece, ⅞ in (2cm) above the edge and 3⅞ in (10cm) apart. Work two 1-in (2.5cm) buttonholes by machine or by hand.

Blanket stitch along the edge of the opening with cream thread, following the inner machined hemline and spacing the stitches ½ in (1cm) apart.

Place the upper back piece over the top edge of the lower back piece, matching up the balance points at the sides. Sew two buttons onto the lower cushion back at the marked points, corresponding with the buttonholes in the upper piece. Do up the buttons and tack both sides of the back piece to secure.

With wrong sides together, pin the front and back of the cushion together, then tack and machine stitch ½-in (1cm) seams round the edges. Machine a parallel stitch line along the outer edge.

Work blanket stitch neatly round the edges of the cushion using six strands of cream thread, following the inner machined hemline as a guide and spacing the stitches ½ in (1cm) apart.

Finishing

Lightly press with a damp cloth (see page 128).

Materials and equipment

For each cushion:
• 19¾ in (50cm) of red wool felt (minimum 52 in/130cm wide)
• 12-in (30cm) square of cream wool felt for the appliqué reindeer or dove and corner hearts
• 4-in (10cm) square of light green wool felt for the appliqué leaves on the dove design only
• Two 2 x 15 in (5 x 38cm) pieces of red cotton for the back opening facings
• Two 2 x 15 in (5 x 38cm) pieces of iron-on interfacing
• Two flat buttons, ⅞ in (2cm) diameter
• 16-in (40cm) square of bonding web
• Reindeer or dove design template (see pages 116 and 117)
• Cushion pattern (see pages 32–3)
• Sharp, hard pencil
• Sewing machine, thread and sewing kit
• 12-in (30cm) embroidery ring
• Embroidery kit and stranded cotton embroidery thread (dyefast) in red and cream for the reindeer, and in red, green, light green and cream for the dove
• Ironing cloth
• 15 x 15 in (38 x 38cm) feather-filled cushion inner

reindeer cushion template

(see cushion pattern on pages 32–3.
Final cushion size 15 x 15 in/38 x 38cm)

Pattern 50%

Pattern 50%

Heart Christmas Stocking

Keep up the wonderful traditions of Christmas with this cheerful stocking. Fill it with wrapped gifts, sweets, chocolates and the ubiquitous yuletide orange. The hearts have been cut away and appliquéd in reverse with blanket stitch.

Stitches
Blanket stitch edging (see page 122).

Preparation and cutting out
Prepare the wool felt fabrics by pressing them (see tips on page 126).

Using a photocopier, enlarge the stocking pattern and the three heart design templates to full size, shown on page 120 at 45 percent.

Referring to the notes on page 127, cut out one back and one front stocking piece in red wool felt. On the stocking front, cut out the three heart shapes as marked on the pattern. Cut out two cuff bands and three hearts in cream wool felt.

Materials and equipment
- 21¾-in (55cm) square of red wool for stocking
- 13⅜ in (35cm) of cream wool felt (minimum 43 in/110cm wide) for appliqué hearts and cuff
- 10 in (25cm) of cream satin ribbon, ⅜ in (7mm) wide, or silky cord, ¼ in (4mm) wide
- Heart design templates (see page 120)
- Stocking pattern (see page 120)
- Sharp, hard pencil
- Sewing machine, thread and sewing kit
- Embroidery kit and stranded cotton embroidery thread (dyefast) in cream and red
- Ironing cloth

christmas stocking template

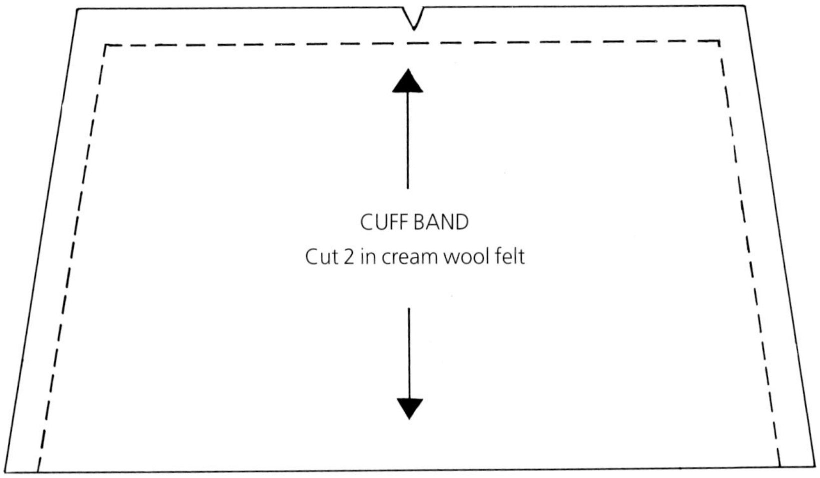

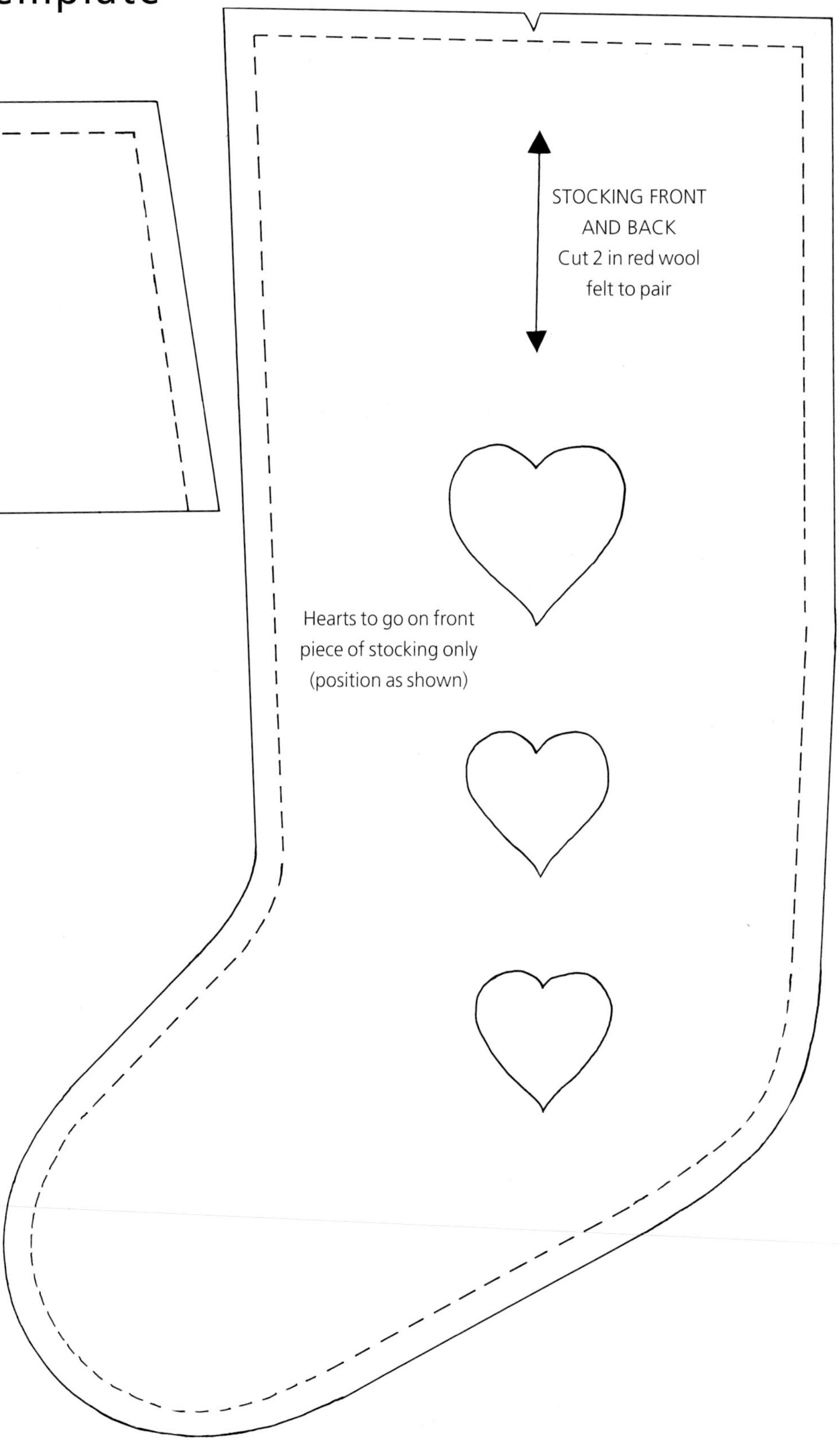

CUFF BAND
Cut 2 in cream wool felt

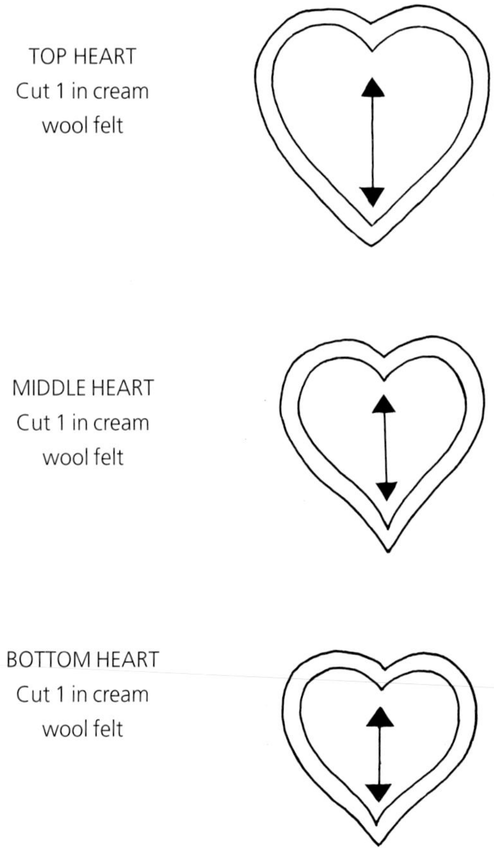

STOCKING FRONT
AND BACK
Cut 2 in red wool
felt to pair

TOP HEART
Cut 1 in cream
wool felt

Hearts to go on front
piece of stocking only
(position as shown)

MIDDLE HEART
Cut 1 in cream
wool felt

BOTTOM HEART
Cut 1 in cream
wool felt

Pattern 45%

Making up and embroidering the stocking

Take the cream heart shapes and pin then tack them into position on the wrong side of the front piece of the stocking, covering the corresponding cutout shapes (see picture 1).

Turn the fabric right side up and embroider the hearts in place by working ¼-in-long (5mm) blanket stitches approximately ⅛ in (4mm) apart round the outlines of the hearts, using six strands of cream thread (see picture 2).

With wrong sides together, join the front and back pieces of the stocking by pinning, tacking and machine stitching a ½-in (1cm) seam allowance round the outer edge. Machine a parallel row of stitching just inside the outer edge.

Work blanket stitch with six strands of cream thread round the edge of the stocking, neatly following the inner machined hemline as a guide and sewing each stitch ½ in (1cm) apart.

To make the stocking cuff, pin, tack and machine stitch the sides of the two pieces together with right sides facing. Press the seams open. Blanket stitch the lower edge of the cuff band using red thread and ½-in-long (1cm) stitches spaced ½ in (1cm) apart.

Attach the cuff band by placing the right side of the cuff onto the wrong side of the stocking, aligning the top edges. Insert a hanging loop at the right-hand side seam, then pin, tack and machine stitch round the top edge (see picture 3).

Fold the cuff band over to the right side of the stocking, so that the top seam is hidden between the two layers. Top stitch ½ in (1cm) in from the edge to hold the cuff band in position.

Finishing

Lightly press with an ironing cloth to finish (see notes on pressing and finishing on page 128).

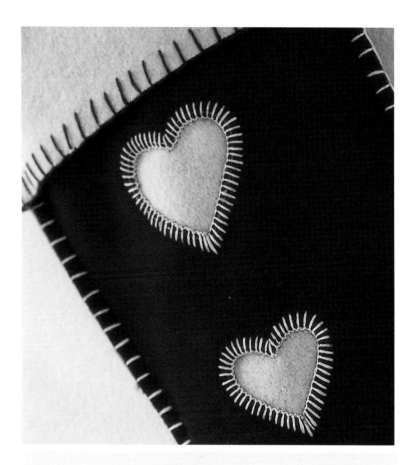

Blanket stitch edging

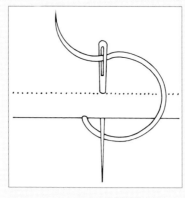

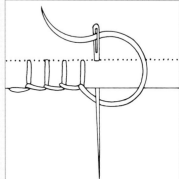

Mark a stitch guideline parallel to the edge. Working from left to right, bring the needle out to the front of the fabric very close to the edge. Put the needle in on the upper line, one space to the right, and bring it through to the front again over the top of the working thread. Continue as required, spacing the stitches evenly along the row. To finish, secure the thread by making a tiny stitch on the edge.

Glossary of Stitches

Blanket stitch

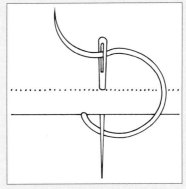 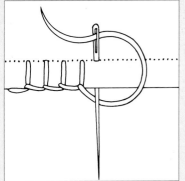

This is the traditional stitch used to edge blankets. It gives a neat finish to raw edges and can be used for appliqué. If the vertical stitches are so close that they are touching, it is known as buttonhole stitch.

Mark a stitch guideline parallel to the edge of the fabric. Working from left to right, bring the needle out to the front of the fabric very close to the edge. Put the needle back in on the upper line, one space to the right, and bring it through to the front again with the tip of the needle over the top of the working thread. Continue as required, spacing the stitches evenly along the row.

To finish, make a tiny stitch on the edge to secure.

Blanket stitch appliqué

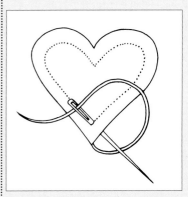 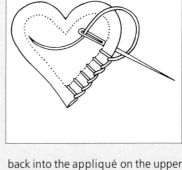

With the appliqué shape secured in place on the main fabric, either by tacking or bonding web, mark an inner stitch guideline parallel to the edge. Working from left to right, bring the needle to the front of the main fabric just below the lower point of the heart, or other appliqué shape. Put the needle back into the appliqué on the upper marked line, one space to the right. Bring the needle straight out again, just below the front edge and over the top of the working thread. Continue as required, spacing the stitches evenly along the row so that they are symmetrical on both sides of the appliqué.

Buttonhole stitch on the round

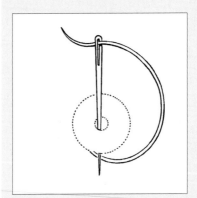 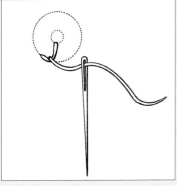 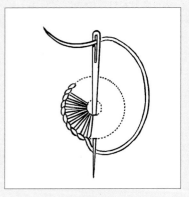

Working from left to right, bring the thread through to the front of the fabric on the lower line, insert the needle on the upper line and make a straight downward stitch, keeping the working thread under the point of the needle.

Pull up the thread to form a loop.

Repeat the stitch all round the circle to form the flower, spacing the stitches evenly as required.

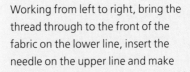

Buttonhole stitch

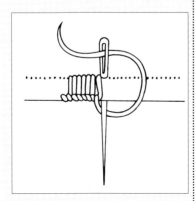

This is the same as blanket stitch, but with the stitches closer together so that no fabric shows between them. It is used for buttonholes, edging and decorative borders.

To use as an edging, mark a guideline parallel to the edge of the fabric and bring the needle out to the front of the fabric on the lower line. Put the needle in on the upper line, slightly to the right, and bring it down and round to the front edge, keeping the working thread under the needle. Continue as required.

Straight stitch

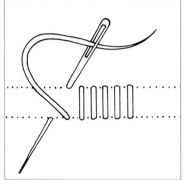

Used for short straight lines, straight stitch can be worked regularly (as shown) or more randomly.

Mark two parallel guidelines. Working from right to left, bring the needle to the front of the fabric on the lower guideline and put it back in directly above on the upper guideline. Bring the needle out again on the lower line one stitch space to the left, as shown.

Repeat and work consistently with the needle always going in on the top line and back out on the bottom.

Running stitch

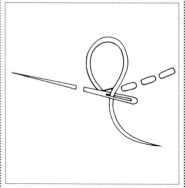

This is the simplest of stitches, made by working stitches of equal lengths in a line. Bring the needle through to the front and then just pick up a few threads of the base fabric in between each stitch.

Stem stitch

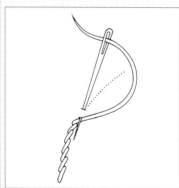

Working from left to right, bring the needle out to the front of the fabric and, slanting a little, put the needle in to the right and bring it back out halfway along the working stitch. Continue as required.

Cross stitch

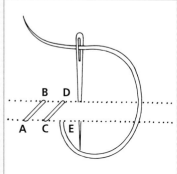 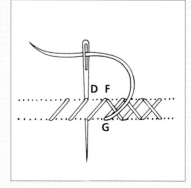

Cross stitch is one of the oldest and best-known embroidery stitches. It is quick to do and very effective, as long as the stitches all run in the same direction and are the same size.

Mark two parallel lines on the fabric. Bring the needle to the front of the fabric at point A. Put the needle in at point B and bring it out again at point C. Then put the needle in again at point D and bring it out at point E, continuing to the end of the row.

For the top row of stitches that complete the crosses, use the same holes and work back. Bring the needle out on the bottom row at point G and put it in at point D. Continue in this way to finish the row.

Slip stitch

This is a sewing stitch used for closing a seam. Turn the seams under and press with an iron. Using matching thread and a regular needle, on one side of the opening begin with a stitch that starts from the inside along the folded edge. Cross to the opposite side, stepping back a little and repeat the stitch. Continue to the end of the seam.

French knot

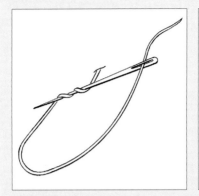 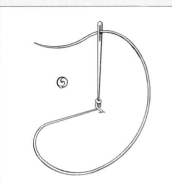

Bring the thread up through the fabric, hold it with the thumb and first finger of the left hand and turn the needle round it once or twice, or as necessary.

Still holding the thread firmly with the left hand, turn the needle and insert it close to the point at which it emerged (not exactly the same place or it will just pull back through). Pull the thread taut so that the knot slides down the needle to touch the fabric. Release the thread as the needle goes through the fabric with the knot remaining on the surface.

Overcast stitch

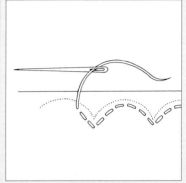 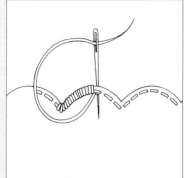

This stitch is used for the scalloped edge on the Strawberry Lavender Sachet (see page 42). Mark the scalloped edge onto the fabric with a fine tailor's chalk pencil. Stitch small running stitches $\frac{1}{16}$–$\frac{1}{8}$ in (2–3mm) from this line. Cut out along the marked line with small sharp scissors. Take the needle over the edge of the fabric and bring it out just to the right, forming very close stitches. Continue as required, keeping a very even tension for a neat finish.

Bullion knot

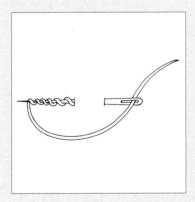 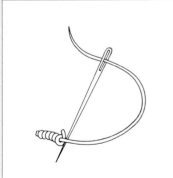 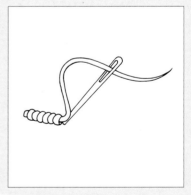

The bullion knot is used singly for the stamens of the lily on the Lily Cushion (see page 84). Bring the needle to the front of the fabric and put the needle back in a short distance away (the required length of the stitch). Bring the needle halfway back out again and coil the thread round the needle six or seven times. Pack the coils down evenly onto the fabric and, holding them with the left thumb, pull the needle and thread through the fabric and the coil, making it lie flat. Insert the needle back into the fabric to secure the knot and finish with a few tiny stitches at the back.

Irregular satin stitch

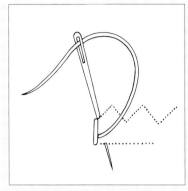

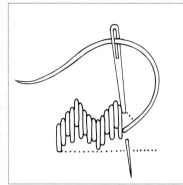

This stitch is similar to long and short stitch with all the stitches worked in the same direction. Work from left to right and top to bottom with straight stitches. Bring out the needle and following the marked outline, put the needle in then out

again, making alternate large and small stitches. Keep the stitches parallel and close together, showing no background fabric, and repeat along the bottom edge, filling in the unstitched areas accordingly.

Loop stitch

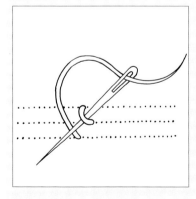

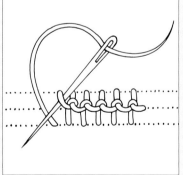

This is used as a straight line to emphasize the wide hem of the napkins and the runner. Mark two parallel lines above and below the hem. Working from right to left, bring the needle up in the center,

put the needle in on the top line and out on the lower line, slightly to the left. Take the needle under the previous stitch from right to left and then over the top of the thread to form the loop. Repeat as required.

Basic satin stitch

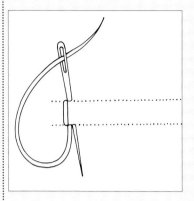

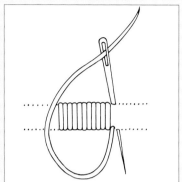

Satin stitch creates a smooth, solid filling for small areas such as flowers and leaves (see below). The tension must be kept even and the stitches quite short to keep them neat. Work

straight stitches close together, taking the needle through the fabric as illustrated. Repeat consistently for a smooth, even finish with no background fabric visible.

Satin stitch

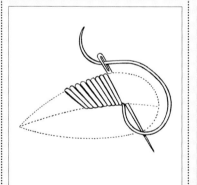

Work straight stitches next to each other, as described above, but at a slant to suit the shape you are filling. For the bottom part of the leaf, lay the stitches next to each other for a smooth and even finish, with no background fabric visible.

Padded satin stitch

This is used for the sunflower on the Cottage Border Tea Cozy and Scarf (see pages 46 and 52) to create a padded effect. Sew running stitch round the center of the circle first and then sew satin stitch over the top. Do this by working straight stitches, taking the needle through as illustrated, and repeat. Work consistently for a smooth, even finish with no background fabric visible.

Chain stitch

One of the oldest and most widely used stitches, chain stitch is used as an outline or a filling stitch by working multiple rows.

Work the chain downwards making a series of loops the same size and not too tight or they will lose their shape. Bring the needle out to the front of the fabric and return it through the same point, bringing it out again to cover the working thread with the needle, forming a loop. Repeat as required and finish the last loop with a tiny straight stitch.

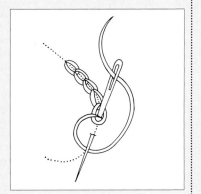

Zigzag chain stitch

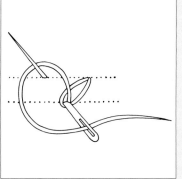
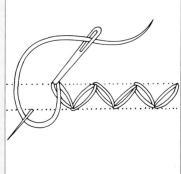

This is a type of chain stitch and is worked between two parallel marked lines.

Bring the needle to the front of the fabric and then put the needle back in at the same place. Bring the needle back out a little to the left on the opposite line, forming the loop by keeping the working thread under the tip of the needle. Put the needle back in again and then bring it out on the opposite line, a little to the left, forming the loop again. Repeat as required.

Notes

Tips – before you start

• Always use the best quality fabrics you can afford, so that the finished embroidered item will last. Traditionally, linen has been the choice of most embroiderers as it is strong and keeps its shape. I have used either linen, a linen/cotton mix or a good quality woven wool with a felted finish for the heavier appliqué projects.

• If you are not an experienced embroiderer, start off with simple projects that are within your capabilities and learn how to handle the fabric and thread. When you have gained confidence in your skills, move on to something a little more challenging.

• Before cutting out, wash and iron the fabric if it is washable (particularly cotton and linen), to ensure that it will not shrink later and ruin the embroidery. This prevents both the embroidery and the seams from puckering if more than one type of fabric is used together. For wool and other fabrics that are not washable, prepare them for embroidery by pressing them well with a cloth placed between the iron and the fabric to prevent the hot iron from making the fabric shiny. Dry clean if necessary once the project is complete.

Embroidery kit

• Embroidery needles
• Stranded cotton thread in the required colors
• Small, sharp embroidery scissors
• Embroidery rings/hoops in various sizes or an embroidery frame

Needles

A fine crewel needle, which has a sharp point and a long eye, has been used for all the projects that use linen and thinner fabrics. A larger chenille needle, which has a larger eye to take thicker thread, can be used for the thicker woollen appliqué projects. Use what you feel comfortable with and, if you can get used to it, work with a thimble to protect your fingers. Needles are graded (1–10) from coarse to fine: the larger the number, the finer the needle.

Threads

Use the stranded cotton variety of thread, which is made up of six strands that can be divided up to give a finer thread. Work with lengths of no more than about 16 in (40cm) to avoid the thread tangling and to stop it from losing its sheen.

Embroidery rings/hoops and frames

Embroidery is easier to handle and the results will be more regular if it is stitched in a ring or a frame; there is also less distortion of the fabric. If you are stitching a large piece of embroidery, it is quite easy to move the ring along the piece once a part of the work has been completed. If the project is very large, then a frame can be used, which can be made by joining four wooden battens at the corners; the fabric can be attached with drawing pins or staples. When using a ring, adjust the screw on the outer ring so that it fits snugly over the inner ring and fabric. Ease it down over the inner ring, pulling the fabric taut and removing any wrinkles. Tighten the screw with a screwdriver.

Sewing kit
- A regular sewing needle
- Cotton sewing thread
- Dressmaker's pins
- Paper scissors
- Sharp dressmaker's shears
- Tape measure and ruler
- Tailor's chalk or water-soluble pen or pencil
- Sewing machine
- Iron and ironing board
- Ironing cloth
- Water spray to dampen cloth

Resizing designs
Many of the patterns for the projects in this book are shown at a percentage of their actual size. The easiest way to enlarge them to full size is on a photocopier.

Cutting out
- Dressmaker's shears (use to cut fabric only)
- Scissors for paper
- Pins
- Tailor's chalk
- Ruler and tape measure

Make sure that the fabric is crease-free and place it on a large, smooth, flat surface. The true grain of the fabric runs down the length, parallel with the edges (selvedges). When placing your pattern onto the fabric, always ensure that the grain line on the pattern is absolutely straight with the grain of the fabric, otherwise the finished item will appear twisted and hang very badly. If you are using the full width of the cloth (for items such as throws and tablecloths), ensure that the selvedges are neatly cut away first, as these are often stretched and have pin holes in them, which are unsightly and unworkable.

Pin the pattern in place on the fabric and, using tailor's chalk, trace neatly round each piece, checking that the straight grain line is parallel with the selvedge. Remove the pins and the pattern to reveal the marked shapes. Cut round the shapes with sharp dressmaker's scissors, just on the inside of the chalk line. It is helpful to look ahead at the line as you cut, to produce more accurately cut pieces.

On some patterns there are balance points and on others there are notches. Both of these guides mean the same and require a ¼ in (5mm) snip to be made at right angles into the edge of the cloth.

If the pattern reads 'cut 2 to pair', cut out one using the pattern the right way up; then turn the pattern over so that it is the wrong way up before cutting out the second. It is necessary to cut fabric to pair when the front of the cloth is different from the back.

Transferring the design
Though there are several methods of transferring the design, the one used throughout this book is with dressmaker's carbon paper. This is available in several colors, so choose one that will show up on the fabric you are using.

Working on a smooth, clean surface, place the carbon paper face down in position on the right side of the fabric and secure it with masking tape. With a sharp, hard pencil, carefully trace round the design, checking to make sure that it is transferring properly.

After the embroidery has been worked, it may be necessary to wash the fabric to remove any remaining visible color.

Embroidering the design
It is advisable to use a ring while embroidering to keep the work flat and in shape and the stitches neat and even. When not embroidering, remove the work from the ring to avoid distortion.

Start a design in the center and work from there towards the left and then towards the right. If the embroidery is large, move the ring around on the fabric, as necessary.

Do not use a knot to fasten the thread at the start of your work, as this can appear lumpy and unsightly; instead, sew two or three backstitches in an area that will be covered by embroidery. Alternatively, leave ⅞ in (2cm) of thread loose at the back and darn this into the embroidery once the work has been completed. To finish, secure the thread at the back with several stitches into an embroidered area, and cut off the thread.

Washing after embroidery
If the embroidered fabric needs to be washed when the stitching has been completed, wash it by hand in warm, soapy water and rinse well. Gently squeeze out the excess water, lay the embroidery face down on a towel and iron, being careful not to scorch it, then leave it to dry. Dry clean any fabrics that are not washable, such as wool.

Pressing finished embroidery
Embroidered fabrics need to be pressed lightly on the back to smooth out the creases and wrinkles that may have been caused by the stitching. Pad out the ironing board with a folded towel and lay the embroidery right side down on it and pull it gently into shape. Cover the embroidery with a damp cotton cloth and go over it lightly with the iron, taking care not to squash any heavily stitched areas or French knots. Allow the embroidery to dry properly.

Using bonding web
This magical product is used throughout the book for appliqué embroidery. It bonds the appliqué shape securely onto the backing fabric, making easy work of the stitching. Using a sharp pencil, trace the design through onto the smooth side of the bonding web (if the design is not symmetrical, it will need to be transferred in reverse). Iron the bonding web onto the wrong side of the appliqué fabric and cut out the shape, cutting on the inside of the traced outline. Peel off the backing and place the shape in the correct position on the base fabric and pin it in place.

Press to seal the shape into position, using a cotton cloth to protect the fabric if necessary, and remove the pins. The shape is now firmly fused in position and can be placed into a ring to be embroidered.

Making up

A basic sewing machine is required for nearly all the projects in the book. Most machines have a zigzag stitch option and this is useful to neaten seams unless an overlocker machine is available.

Use a ½-in (1cm) seam throughout the projects in the book, unless otherwise specified. Wherever the instructions are to pin, tack and machine stitch, remember to remove all the tacking stitches once the machine stitching has been completed.

Always snip off any corners to reduce bulk before turning through. Similarly, also taper away some of the seam allowance if the seam is on a curve to give a better shape once the fabric is turned right side out.

Making bias strips for piping

To make bias strips, you need a large square of fabric. Fold a straight raw edge parallel to the selvedge to form a triangle. Using tailor's chalk and a long ruler, mark out a series of parallel lines to the required width (1¼ in/3cm). Cut out and join the strips end to end to make a long strip, and press the seams flat.

Fold the bias strip in half over the piping cord and pin, tack and machine stitch to close the strip, encasing the cord snugly.

To secure, place the piping along the seam line and pin, tack and machine stitch it to one side of the article. When stitching round corners, lift the presser foot of the machine at the corner and swivel the fabric round, then lower the presser foot and carry on stitching the next edge – repeating on all the corners.

Where the piped edges meet, cut down the cord so that the ends butt together. Trim the ends of the fabric strips so that they overlap by ½ in (1cm),

turning under ½ in (1cm) on the visible top strip and tucking the opposite raw edge underneath.

Attach the other side of the article by putting right sides together. Pin, tack and machine stitch, using the line of stitching already sewn to attach the piping as a guide.

Trim the corners and clip the edge of the piping if necessary to allow ease. Turn the article right sides out and press lightly round the edges with the tip of the iron.

Pressing the finished item

Once an article has been completed, press it to give a neat finish, using the recommended heat setting. For wool, use an ironing cloth between the fabric and the iron to prevent shine on the surface. The finished piece should be laid right side down on an ironing board. Be very careful not to flatten the texture of the embroidery. Use steam, if necessary, or a damp cloth to remove any stubborn creases.

Acknowledgments

Thank you to everyone who has helped me to put this book together:

Jacqui Small for giving me the opportunity to write this book.
Joanna Copestick and Zia Mattocks for being such patient editors.
Maria Bowers for designing the layout so happily.
Caroline Arber for her beautiful photography.
Estelle Corke for her lovely embroidery paintings.
Jo, Suzanne, Meenakshi, Sharon, Pankaj and Charlotte for their help with the projects.
The girls in my office for holding the fort while I wrote.
Elaine Constantine, my sister, for giving so much.

To my husband, David, for all his help and support at home and away.
And my daughters, Camille and Mary, for their enthusiasm.

Sources

Usually, you can find the supplies you need for making the projects in Lark books at your local craft supply store, discount mart, home improvement center, or retail shop relevant to the topic of the book. Occasionally, however, you may need to buy materials or tools from specialty suppliers. In order to provide you with the most up-to-date information, we have created a listing of suppliers on our website, which we update on a regular basis. Visit us at www.larkbooks.com, click on "Sources," and then search for the relevant materials. You can also search by book title, vendor, and author name. Additionally, you can search for supply sources located in or near your town by entering your zip code. You will find numerous companies listed, with the web address and/or mailing address and phone number.